RobotBASIC Projects for the Parallax Scribbler S3

John Blankenship

Table of Contents

Chapter 1
Introduction to Programming with RobotBASIC

I helped develop the programming language RobotBASIC with Samuel Mishal (easily the greatest programmer I have ever known). We made it extremely easy to use even though it is a powerful tool for controlling robots, writing simple video games, and learning about programming in general. RobotBASIC runs on a standard PC running the FULL Windows' operating system (not RT), not on Apple products or Android tablets and phones unless you have a really good emulator. Since our primary goal for writing RobotBASIC was to increase student interest in engineering and programming, we give it away free to students, schools, teachers, and hobbyists (visit www.RobotBASIC.org). There are no purchasing costs, no site licenses, and no upgrade fees – EVER! RobotBASIC truly is free and RobotBASIC is easier to use and much more powerful than most educational languages.

The RobotBASIC IDE
Figure 1.1 shows the Integrated Development Environment (IDE) for RobotBASIC. There are drop-down menus across the top with a variety of short-cut buttons below. The green triangle button is the short-cut to run programs. Various features of RobotBASIC will be introduced as needed throughout this book but you can always get detailed information on everything in RobotBASIC by clicking the **?** button to read the HELP file. Note: The HELP file must be in the same directory as RobotBASIC itself.

RobotBASIC's Simulated Robot
One of the great things about RobotBASIC is its integrated robot simulator. The short program in Figure 1.2 shows how easily you can control the simulation. The first line in the program creates the simulated robot by locating it at screen position 400,300. Since the output screen is 800 by 600, the robot is created in the center of the screen.   All robot related commands in RobotBASIC begin with the letter **r**. Think of **rLocate** as *Robot Locate*.

The second line in the program slows the robot down so it is easier to watch. The parameter is a delay time, so zero is the fastest with larger numbers producing slower movements. The third line drops a pen so that the robot leaves a trail as it moves. Leaving a trail will be used often in this book to make it easier for you to follow what the robot is doing.

The next 3 lines move the robot forward 40 units, turn it right 90⁰, and move it forward again 80 units. For the simulator, the units are screen pixels. Since the robot is 40 pixels in diameter, the first move is a distance equal to the robot's diameter. The second move is twice the robot's diameter.

NOTE: Some images in this text, due to the printing process used, are not quite as clear as we would like and many are easier to view in color. For these reasons, the download ZIP file from RobotBASIC.org for this book includes a PDF containing color images of most non-text figures that can be viewed with your computer.

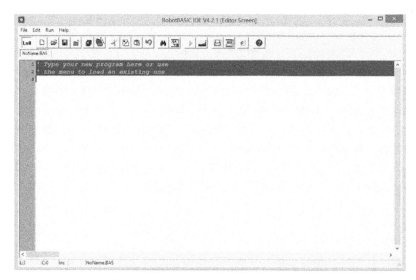

Figure 1.1: RobotBASIC's IDE

```
rLocate 400,300
rSpeed 10
rPen DOWN
rForward 40
rTurn 90
rForward 80
end
```
Figure 1.2: This program leaves a trail as it moves the simulated robot.

Once you have the programmed typed in, you can run it by clicking the green triangle. If you have typed the program in correctly, you will see the robot move as shown in Figure 1.3. Notice the output window pops up in front of the IDE. As expected, the robot is initialized in the center of the screen and faces upward by default (considered north to the simulator).

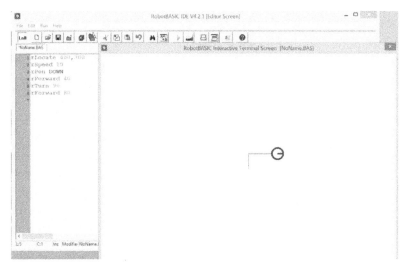

Figure 1.3: When you run the program in Figure 1.2, the robot responds as shown.

The trail left by the robot as it moves shows that the robot initially moved a distance approximately equal to its diameter before turning right and moving twice its diameter. The simulator may look unsophisticated, but it has many exciting capabilities that will be explored in later chapters. The important point is that RobotBASIC makes controlling the simulation extremely easy. Wouldn't it be nice if controlling a real robot could be just as easy?

The Parallax Scribbler S3
Throughout this book we will be using the real robot shown in Figure 1.4. It is the Scribbler robot (the S3 model) from Parallax (www.Parallax.com). A RobotBASIC controlled Scribbler is one of the easiest and most enjoyable ways to learn about programming a robot.

Figure 1.4: The Parallax S3 robot can be controlled by RobotBASIC.

This book assumes the reader has no programming experience so the complexities of the projects will start slowly and build throughout the book, culminating with the S3 completing interesting tasks without human intervention. Chapter 2 will explain how to modify the S3 so we can control it with the same commands used to control RobotBASIC's simulated robot. The modifications require no tools and no soldering. For now though, let's continue our introduction to programming.

Errors

If you made a typing error when you entered the program in Figure 1.2, it will not respond as expected. If, for example, you typed **rForward 4** instead of **rForward 40**, the robot would travel only a small amount on its first move. Errors like this require you to watch the robot's behavior to see if it actually does what you want it to do. When it does not, you can mentally trace through the program after watching the simulation to discover the offending statement. The important point is that the program will do what *you tell it to do*, not necessarily what you *want it to do*.

Sometimes a typo can create a situation that RobotBASIC cannot perform at all. Suppose, for example that you entered **Turn 90** instead of **rTurn 90**. RobotBASIC does not have an instruction called **Turn**, so it stops trying to run the program when it encounters that word and provides an error message (see Figure 1.5) indicating *what it thinks the problem might be*. Notice that all the statements encountered before the error were executed correctly.

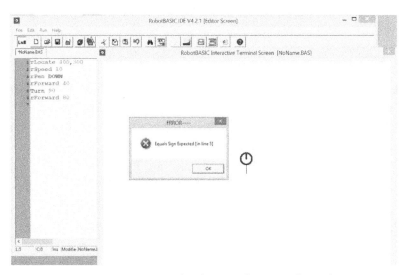

Figure 1.5: Some errors are bad enough to confuse the system.

Error Messages

The error message in Figure 1.5 is not really correct because it did not say "You misspelled **rTurn**". That would have been nice, but as you experiment with RobotBASIC (or any other programming language) you will see that *it does not know what you are trying to do*, so it just makes a *reasonable guess* at what *might* be wrong.

Variables

In this case, RobotBASIC thinks you might have been assigning a value to a variable named **Turn**. To make this clearer, let's explore variables for a moment before continuing. Assume we have a program like the one in Figure 1.6. It assigns a value of 22 to a variable named **X** and a value of 3.5 to the variable **Y**. The third line in the program adds **X** and **Y** together and stores the result in the variable **dog**. The final line will print 25.5 on the output screen. Enter this program and run it to verify it works.

Most computer languages require that you specify, in advance, if a particular variable will be used for integers or floating point numbers. RobotBASIC lets you store integers and floats (even strings of characters) in any variable at any time (and change them at any time too).

```
X = 22
Y = 3.5
dog = X+Y
print dog
```

Figure 1.6: Variables make mathematics easy.

Case Sensitivity

Sometimes using the wrong capitalization can be interpreted by RobotBASIC as a typo or a misspelling. Commands in RobotBASIC are *not* case sensitive. You can, for example, use **rForward** or **rforward** or **RFORWARD** – all will work the same. Since any type of capitalization will work with commands, you can use whatever makes the program easier for you to read. You might like the choices used throughout this book, but you can use your own preferences when it comes to commands.

Variables though, are different. As you can see from Figure 1.6, variables can be a single letter like **X** or **Y** or even **A** or **M**. You can also use words or any combination of letters like **dog** or **Cat** or even **abc**. You can use numbers too, as long as the variable starts with a letter (like **A3** or **answer6**). Usually a programmer will name variables something that indicates what the variable is being used for. For example, instead of **dog**, it might have made more sense in this program to use a name like **sum** or **Answer**. You can use any name you want, as long as it is not a command. For example, you could not have a variable called **print** or **rForward** because these are commands in RobotBASIC. And don't forget, variables are case sensitive, so **Y** and **y** are *different* variables as are **dog** and **Dog**.

Back to Error Messages

Look back at Figure 1.5. In this case, RobotBASIC did not recognize **Turn** as a command, so it *assumed* it was a variable. Once it made that assumption, it then assumed you were trying to assign it a value of 90, which is why the error message indicated an equal sign was expected (RobotBASIC *thought* you were trying to write **Turn = 90**). It was wrong of course, but it was making a *reasonable guess* at what might be a way to fix the error.

Notice also in Figure 1.5 that it tells you the error is in line 5 and if you look at the line numbers to the left of the program you will see the error is indeed in line 5. If you close the error box by clicking the **OK** button, the error box and the output window will both disappear and line 5 in the editor will be highlighted. Effectively, RobotBASIC is taking you directly to the offending line so that you can correct the problem.

Of course, as we have seen, you cannot assume that RobotBASIC is always right when it tells you what it thinks the error is. It is up to you to look at the output from the program and the offending line and decide on your own what the error really is. Sometimes the error might not even be in the line that RobotBASIC thinks caused the error. As you learn more about programming, you will learn more about errors and how to find and correct them.

More about Programming

Normally, when a program is run, the statements are executed in order, starting at the beginning and continuing until an **END** statement is reached or until there are no more statements left in the program.

The real power of programming however, is its ability to alter the order that statements are executed. Perhaps a few examples can help make this clearer. Let's assume we want to write a program to print all the numbers from 1 to 30. We could write a program that is made up of 30 **PRINT** statements. The first would be **PRINT 1**, the second **PRINT 2**, and so on – ending with **PRINT 30**. Typing in so many statements would take a while, but it would work. Fortunately, there is a better way. Look at the program in Figure 1.7.

```
for n = 1 to 30
  print n
next
end
```

Figure 1.7: Loops (as shown here) can make programming more efficient.

The program in Figure 1.7 is composed of a **FOR-NEXT** loop. The **FOR** is the beginning of the loop and the **NEXT** is the end. Every line in between will be executed over and over (based on the information in the **FOR** statement. In this example, the **FOR** is told to make the variable **n** start with a value of 1 before beginning the loop. Inside the loop, the current value of **n** (which is 1 initially) is printed and then the **NEXT** is executed. Each time the **NEXT** executes, it increases the value of **n** by 1 and the loop is started over with the first line following the **FOR** statement. This means the first time through the loop **n** is 1, the second time through **n** is 2 etc. This looping continues as long as the value of **n** does not exceed 30. Eventually, when **n** exceeds 30, the loop terminates and execution continues with the line following the **NEXT**. Type in this program and run it to see that it does print all the numbers from 1 to 30.

STEP

As with many statements in RobotBASIC, the **FOR** has options. If you replace it with the following line, you will see that the program will only print *odd* numbers. If you started the loop with 2 (instead of 1) it would only print *even* numbers.

```
for n = 1 to 30 step 2
```

The **STEP** option tells the **NEXT** to increase the value of **n** by 2, not 1 as before. This causes the program to print the numbers 1, 3, 5..... 27, 29. Try it. What do you think would happen if you used **STEP 3**? Try it to see if you are right.

Add a second **PRINT** line as shown below. Insert the new **PRINT** right *after* the first one in the program, but before the **NEXT**.

```
print 0
```

With both statements inside the loop, the program will now print the numbers 1, 0, 2, 0, 3, 0 etc. Study the program to see why this should happen. Again, try this on your computer to verify it is true. When you have verified everything, erase the old program and type in the one in Figure 1.8.

```
for n = 1 to 30 step 2
   print "The value of N is ",n
   print "--------------------"
next
end
```

Figure 1.8: This program demonstrates the **FOR-NEXT** loop.

This program demonstrates that you can print text (a *string* of characters) by simply placing it inside quotes. The first **PRINT** statement prints the sentence **The value of N is** and then it prints the actual value of the variable **n** on the same line. Notice the space after **is** inside the quotes. Why is it necessary? Remove it and run the program to see why it is necessary.

The second **PRINT** in the program displays a series of dash marks or negative signs. Figure 1.9 shows what the output will be if you run this program. Your output window may be in a different place, but you can move it just as you do any window on a PC. Notice also that the **N** is capitalized inside the *string* of characters. This has no effect on the variable **n** inside program because the **N** is just text to be printed and not related to the variable **n**.

Hopefully these simple examples have piqued your interest in programming. Future chapters will introduce different kinds of loops as well as structures that allow your programs to make decisions about *what* and *when* things should be done. Before the end of the book, we will use such statements to write programs that allow a robot (both the S3 and the simulated robot) to make decisions on its own as it works to accomplish the goals we set for it.

Don't worry if you feel a little confused at this point. If you are new to programming, a little confusion is normal. Things will become clearer as you see more programs and even more so when you experiment with them on your own. Let's move on to Chapter 2 to see how the S3 can be modified to work with RobotBASIC.

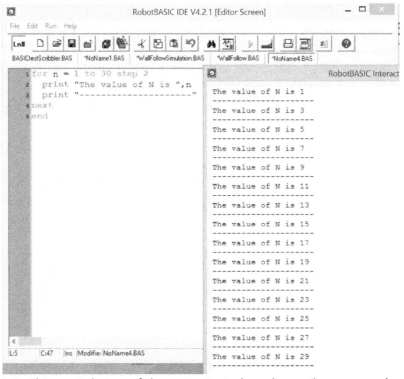

Figure 1.9: This partial view of the output window shows the program's output.

Chapter 2
Enhancing the S3

This chapter moves us toward our goal of being able to control the Parallax Scribbler S3 from RobotBASIC. The S3 was chosen for this book because it one of the few fully-assembled educational robots with a decent variety of sensors. Sensors are very important because they allow a robot to interact with its environment. The more sensors a robot has, the more options we have for creating interesting and motivational projects.

The RobotBASIC Experience
Controlling the S3 from RobotBASIC is a totally different experience than programming it with other languages from Parallax such as Spin or BlocklyProp. With RobotBASIC your programs can utilize fixed, float, and string variables (both local and global). You have access to extensive graphics capable of flicker-free animation, multi-dimensional arrays, both traditional and graphical user interfaces, an integrated robot simulator, and hundreds of unique functions that make programming easier than ever. But, there is one difference that makes programming the S3 very unique.

Normally when you program the S3 you have to edit your program on an external computer and then download the compiled code to the S3 using a USB cable. If there are errors when the program runs, you typically have to edit the program to fix the mistake, reattach the cable, and download it again. Often these actions must be repeated many times before a working program is achieved. This process is time consuming at best, and often annoying when you are trying to get your program working.

With RobotBASIC you never have to download your program. You just write it and it can *immediately* control the robot. In order to control the Scribbler from RobotBASIC we need to make a few modifications. Most of the modifications are simple and easy, but the more modifications we make, the more powerful the S3 will be. It is suggested that you read through this Chapter completely before making any modifications to your S3.

The modifications come in several complexities. If you only want to utilize the sensors built into the S3 then you only need to add Bluetooth communication. This easy and inexpensive modification will let the S3 handle, on some level, most of the projects in this book. Without additional sensors, though, you will have to make compromises and accept reduced performance for some projects. For many schools with limited robotic curriculums, adding Bluetooth is the only modification they will need.

If you add just one Parallax Ping sensor (also easy) the S3 will be able to measure the distances to objects and that gives you options for more projects. Adding a total of 3 Ping sensors provides the capabilities needed for even more exciting projects and greatly improves the sensor interface. If that is not enough, there will even be suggestions for customizations appropriate for advanced users. Check www.RobotBASIC.org for information about kits and parts needed for the S3 enhancement.

More advanced readers interested in maximizing their S3's performance can add a beacon detector or even augment their robot with custom sensors. Let's examine what is required for these various modifications.

Bluetooth

The minimum modification needed for your S3 is to give it the ability to communicate with RobotBASIC over a Bluetooth link. Most modern PC's, especially laptops and tablet computers, have a built-in Bluetooth interface. If yours does not, you will have to add a USB Bluetooth adapter to your computer. You will also need to add Bluetooth capability to the S3 itself. This can be accomplished with a Bluetooth transceiver (available from RobotBASIC) such as the one in Figure 2.1.

Figure 2.1: A Bluetooth transceiver can allow the S3 to communicate with RobotBASIC.

Only four wires are needed to connect the transceiver to the Hacker Port on the S3 as shown in Figure 2.2. If this is the only modification you are going to make, you can use four female-to-female cables and simply tape or hot-glue the transceiver to the top of the S3 as shown in Figure 2.3.

Transceiver Pin	to	Hacker Port Pin
RXD (receive)		P1
TXD (transmit)		P0
VCC (5 volts)		5V
GND (ground)		G

Figure 2.2: Bluetooth Connections

Figure 2.3: If Bluetooth is your only modification, 4 cables are all you need.

A Single Ping Sensor

If your long-range plans are to add only one Ping sensor, you can attach a solderless breadboard to your S3 with double-stick tape and insert the Bluetooth transceiver into the breadboard as shown in Figure 2.4. You can then make the Bluetooth connections of Figure 2.2 using four male-to-female cables. The male ends simply plug into any of the four holes connected to each of the transceiver pins.

Figure 2.4 also shows the Ping sensor plugged into the breadboard. It can be connected with three male-to-female cables as outlined in Figure 2.5. Always take great care in making hacker-port connections properly. **Making a wrong connection for any component can easily damage the device being interfaced or even the S3 itself**.

Figure 2.4: Mounting a small breadboard on the S3 makes it easy to interface a Bluetooth transceiver and a Ping sensor.

Ping Pin	to	Hacker Port Pin
GND (ground)		G
5V (5 volts)		5V
SIG (signal)		P3

Figure 2.5: Single Ping Connections

Three Ping Expansion

The previous expansions are inexpensive and easy to implement. You can *greatly improve* your S3's capabilities though, by adding a total of three Ping sensors. The biggest expense of adding three Pings is the cost of the Pings themselves, but for serious experimenters, this modification provides several advantages that justify the expense. Just being able to scan the entire area in front of the robot without having to turn the robot is a huge benefit for autonomous navigation. The ability to look to the left while moving forward makes behaviors such as wall-following possible and that can lead to more interesting projects. Finally, multiple Pings make it possible to create a Virtual Sensory System (VSS) that lets you write programs that can quickly and efficiently detect objects in the robot's environment. The VSS is covered in Chapter 9.

The biggest physical problem with adding three Pings is mounting them. You could build something with balsa wood or even just hot glue the sensors directly to the top of the S3. This can work of course (my first prototype used a wood mount for the Pings and is pictured in Figure 2.6) but I wanted something that was sturdy and had a more finished look. For that reason, I arranged to have a mount produced with 3D printing (Figure 2.7). It holds the 3 Pings in the proper positions and provides room for the breadboard. Figure 2.8 shows the mount attached to the S3 with double-sided tape (see Figure 2.9). Notice the Ping sensors in the mount and the breadboard (also attached with double-sided tape. The breadboard actually helps to hold the Pings in place, so make sure they are installed *before* the breadboard.

Figure 2.6: My first prototype.

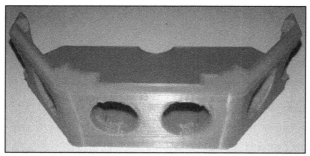

Figure 2.7: This 3D-printed mount makes it easy to install the Ping sensors in the proper orientation.

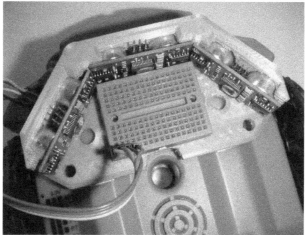

Figure 2.8: The mount with Pings and breadboard. Note the wires for the Bluetooth transceiver.

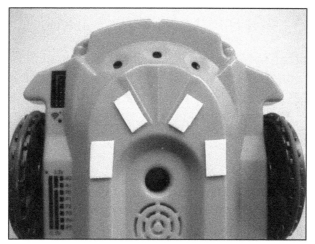

Figure 2.9: The mount is easily attached to the S3 with four small pieces of double-sided tape.

Wiring Three Pings

The pins on the Ping are ground, 5V, and signal, in that order. The pins on the S3 Hacker Port can be viewed in exactly the same order (across the Hacker Port) for P2, P3, and P4. This means we can use standard servomotor cables to connect each of the Pings to the Hacker Port. Just connect the *right-side Ping to P2*, the *center Ping to P3*, and the *left-side Ping to P4*. If you use 3-pin servo cables, each cable connects the 5V power, ground, and control signal simultaneously. Just plug one end into the Hacker Port and connect the other to the appropriate Ping. Make sure the same wire (typically black) connects to the ground pin on both ends. If you do not have three servo cables, you can use nine single wire female-to-female cables. As always, carefully check your wiring for errors before turning on the S3. Note: Appropriate cables come with the kits from RobotBASIC. Figure 2.10 shows the three Pings and the Bluetooth transceiver wired to the Hacker Port.

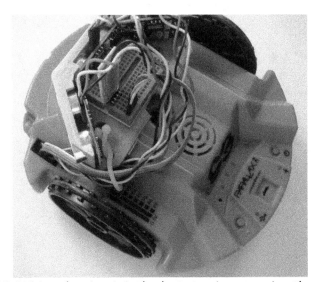

Figure 2.10: Wiring the circuit is the last step in preparing the hardware.

NOTE: At the time of publication for this book, Parallax has just announced a new LASER version of their Ping sensor. Visit the **SCRIBBLER S3** Tab at RobotBASIC.org for information on utilizing the LaserPing with a RROSS-based S3. Don't assume that the new sensor will be preferred over the standard Ping sensor. The LaserPing does have some advantages, but it also has limitations when compared to the original. Read a full analysis on our webpage.

Beacon Detection

The ability to detect beacons can be valuable for many advanced projects. You might, for example, have a beacon behind each goal on an S3-sized soccer field. The actual detector is shown in Figure 2.11. It plugs into the breadboard (Figure 2.12) and is wired to the Hacker Port pin P5 and power as shown in Figure 2.13. Appendix B provides detailed instructions for constructing the actual beacons and Chapters 10 and 12 have projects utilizing a beacon.

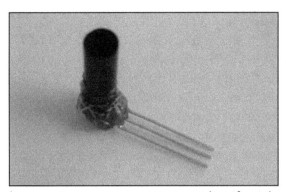

Figure 2.11: The RobotBASIC Beacon Detector can identify eight different beacons.

Figure 2.12: The detector plugs into the breadboard and faces forward to identify beacons.

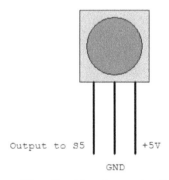

Figure 2.13: Beacon Pins (looking from the front, into the tube)

More Advanced Options

Advanced users can make even more modifications, but the ones described in this chapter should be sufficient for most schools and hobbyists. Appendix A offers suggestions and the technical information needed for further customizing your RobotBASIC controlled S3.

Downloading the RROSS Software

With the hardware complete, the next step is to upload the **RobotBASIC Robot Operating System** for the **S**cribbler (RROSS) to the S3. Simply follow Parallax's instructions for programming the S3 with BlocklyProp. You can obtain the RROSS file from RobotBASIC.org or from Parallax.com. You only have to do this once. Once installed in the S3, the RROSS will run every time the S3 is turned on. Parallax makes it easy to revert your S3 to its standard programming, but once you have used RobotBASIC with you S3, you won't want to go back. For now, don't worry about how the RROSS works. Everything will be revealed shortly.

Chapter 3
Controlling the Robot's Movements

At this point in the book, it is assumed you have enhanced your S3 with at least the Bluetooth capability as discussed in Chapter 2. This means your S3 is ready to be controlled with RobotBASIC. Before we start though, we need to revisit RobotBASIC's simulated robot. In the real world, companies often use computer simulations to speed the development process. As you will soon see, RobotBASIC's simulated robot can make it easier to write and develop programs that control the S3.

A Simulator Program
The program in Figure 3.1 will make RobotBASIC's simulated robot move in various shape patterns like triangles, squares, octagons, etc. Use the RobotBASIC editor to enter the program and set the variable **NumSides** equal to the number of sides you want your shape to have. If you want a triangle, for example, set the number of sides to 3.

The second line in the program prints the characters inside the quotes exactly as written followed by the value of **NumSides**. As you will see, this is a nice touch because it lets the output screen show the user the number of sides being drawn. Next, the variable **TurnAngle** is set to **360/NumSides**. This value will be used to control how much the robot should turn at each of the corners of the polygon it is drawing.

Note: In this program when you divide **360/NumSides**, the answer will be an integer because both numbers in the expression are integers (if an expression is composed entirely of integers, RobotBASIC will automatically perform integer math when evaluating the expressions). For example, 360/7 will be 51, but 360.0/7 will be 51.4285714285714. If you want floating point math, simply use at least one float in the expression to be evaluated.

Integer math is fine in this case, because the simulated robot cannot turn less than one degree anyway. This means, however, that some shapes (7 or 11 sides, for example) will not be perfect due to rounding errors. Slightly more advanced programs could fix this problem, but this version will do for beginners.

Once the robot is located on the screen at pixel position 100,300 (100 across and 300 down), a simulated pen is dropped so the robot will leave a trail as it moves, but there is also a new command that can specify one or more invisible colors. The first invisible color in the list (**GREEN** in this case) is automatically used for the pen. Making this color *invisible* is essential in this program because the robot returns to its original position during its movement and this would cause the robot to travel over the line it has previously drawn. If the line is not invisible, the robot will see it as an object on the screen and colliding with it will cause an error. Future chapters will discuss this idea in far more detail and utilize this feature to help create exciting projects.

```
NumSides = 9
print "Number of sides = ",NumSides
TurnAngle = 360/NumSides
rLocate 100,300
rInvisible GREEN
rPen DOWN
for i=1 to NumSides
  rForward 100
  rTurn TurnAngle
next
rPen UP
rForward 150
print "All Done"
```
Figure 3.1: This program lets the simulated robot draw shapes.

Loops in Programming

The real work of moving the robot is handled by a **FOR-NEXT** loop. As mentioned in Chapter 1, most programs are full of loops that perform a series of actions over and over. Remember, the **FOR** statement marks the beginning of the loop and the **NEXT** marks the end of it. The **FOR** starts by setting the variable specified (**i** in this case) equal to 1. It then executes the statements that follow the **FOR** until it gets to the **NEXT**.

When the **NEXT** is executed, the variable initialized by the **FOR** will be incremented. If the new value is less than or equal to **NumSides** (see the **FOR** statement), then the statements inside the loop are executed again. The variable **i** will be incremented every time through the loop. When the value of **i** becomes greater than **NumSides,** the program will *terminate the loop* and continue execution with the line following the **NEXT** (or terminate the entire program if **NEXT** is the last line in the program. In this case, the robot raises the pen so as to not leave a trail, and moves away from the drawing before printing the phrase **All Done**. Notice the phrase "All Done" (often called a *string* in programming, as in a string of characters) is in quotes to prevent RobotBASIC from thinking it is a variable name or a command.

Inside the **FOR**-loop we see the commands that actually move the robot. Recall that you can move the robot forward with the **rForward** command (backward with negative numbers). The unit of movements for the simulator is pixels (the robot is 40 pixels in diameter). You can turn right a specified number of degrees (or left with negative numbers) with **rTurn**.

Look carefully at the format of the program in Figure 3.1. Notice that the code inside the **FOR-NEXT** control structure (*construct* for short) is indented. The indenting helps you see where the code inside a loop begins and ends. Such organization is NOT required, but it does make programs far easier to read and understand – not just for you but for anyone else reading your code. Companies that hire programmers generally require them to follow company-specified formats so that all programs within the company have the same look and feel. This practice has proven to make programmers more productive and the whole programming process more efficient.

Run the Program

If you set the number of sides to 6 and run the program, you will see the output shown in Figure 3.2. Type in the program on your computer and run the program to watch the robot actually draw the shape specified by **NumSides**. If you want to save your program, you can do so through the FILE menu or with the diskette icon. Notice also that once the drawing is complete, the robot moves away so you can see the entire shape.

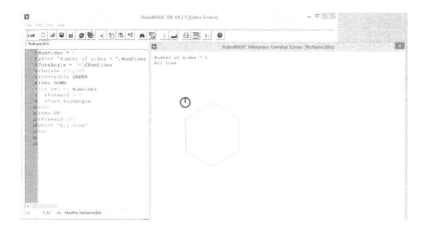

Figure 3.2: The simulated robot can draw.

If you try to create shapes with 14 or more sides, the shape will be so large that the robot will collide with a wall, causing an error (the edge of the screen is consider to be a wall around the robot's environment). This can easily be fixed by reducing the distance traveled by the robot on each pass through the loop. For example, change **rForward 100** to **rForward 50**.

Modifying the Program

Now that you know a little about RobotBASIC, it is time for you to start experimenting with programming – especially if you have never programmed before. In addition to modifying the value of **NumSides**, try reducing the distance the robot travels or changing the invisible color. You can use things like **RED, BLUE, YELLOW, CYAN, BROWN, and GRAY**. RobotBASIC can actually produce thousands of colors, but this is enough for now. Add the statement **LineWidth 10** to the beginning of the program and run it to see what happens. Try all of the above ideas and examine the shapes drawn. Study your modified programs to make sure you see why your changes produced the results you see.

Try to modify the program so it draws a circle. **Hint**: Reduce the length of travel and increase the number of sides. You might even try to locate the robot so that it starts at a different place on the screen. Don't worry if your program produces errors or if you start having a lot of questions. Your experimenting cannot damage RobotBASIC. The worst thing that might happen is that you'll get excited about programming and become impatient to explore future chapters.

The Simulator vs a Real Robot

You may well be wondering why all this discussion on the simulator because you bought this book to learn how to control the S3. Let's modify the program in Figure 3.1 so it can make the Scribbler robot move in a multi-sided pattern, just like the simulator. Using a simulator is great because it allows you to get your program working without having a real robot bumping into walls or raging out of control. We will allow the program to control the S3 only after it successfully controls the simulation. This is a powerful idea you should not take lightly.

Using a simulator also a great way for schools to teach robotics without spending a lot of money. Since RobotBASIC is free, every student can program their own simulated robot (both at school and at home) and then when someone gets their program working, they can use their program to control a real robot. This means a school can buy only a few robots per classroom, even just one if they are on a very tight budget. In fact, if a school (or hobbyist) has extremely limited funds, they can perform most of the projects in this book using only the simulator.

The program in Figure 3.3 will make the S3 draw shapes just like the simulator. Let's look at the code in Figure 3.3 to see how it is different. First of all, notice that that the program is nearly identical to the one in Figure 3.1. The only additions to the program are shown in **BOLD**. Both of these additions involve the Bluetooth transceiver needed for communication between the S3 and RobotBASIC.

```
PortNum = 5 // set to YOUR Bluetooth Port Number
NumSides = 5
print "Number of sides = ",NumSides
TurnAngle = 360/NumSides
rCommPort PortNum // must come before rLocate
rLocate 100,300  // for the S3, the position is ignored
for i=1 to NumSides
  rForward 40
  rTurn TurnAngle
next
print "All Done"
```

Figure 3.3: This program will cause either the simulator
or a real robot to move in a polygon shape.

Pairing the S3 with Your PC

The Bluetooth transceiver on the S3 needs to be *paired* with the Bluetooth hardware on your PC (it should appear as HC-06 in your Windows' menus). The exact steps for pairing Bluetooth devices depends on your operating system (Windows Vista, 8.1, etc.) so refer to the documentation for your computer. When you tell your computer you want to add a Bluetooth device (the adapter on the S3, see Figure 2.1 in Chapter 2) it will ask you for a pairing code. The code for the units available from RobotBASIC is **1234**.

You only have to pair the robot and PC once (unless you change the adapter on the S3 or use a different PC). When the pairing is complete, your system should provide you with the port number used for the Bluetooth communication. For my computer, the port used is 5 and that will be reflected in programs throughout this book. You need to determine *your* port number though and use it instead of 5.

Once you set the variable **PortNum** equal to the port used on your machine, the second bold statement in the program tells RobotBASIC that communication should be handled over the specified port. Note: You could have eliminated the variable **PortNum** and just made the second line **rCommPort 5** and the program would have worked fine. Writing programs this way as programs get bigger though, would mean that you might have to search through your program (to change the port number) each time you wanted to control a different robot (assuming, for example, your school has several S3's, each with their own Bluetooth transceiver and port number). With the variable **PortNum** at the beginning of the code, it is easy to make the change.

The important point is that if you have a program written for the simulator, it can be used with the S3 with minor changes. Once the **rCommPort** has been set up properly, the **rLocate** statement will initialize the S3 (not the simulated robot). The S3 will beep when it is initialized, and it does not care what position is specified the locate statement.

As our programs get more complicated, there will be more changes, but converting a program to work with the S3 is generally easy. If you compare the programs in Figure 3.1 and 3.3, you will also notice that the statements related to the PEN (**rPen** and **rInvisible**) have been removed because they are not needed for the S3. It is important to know though, that the program will run fine even if these lines were not removed. RobotBASIC has been designed to automatically ignore program statements that only apply to the simulation when controlling a real robot.

Try the program in Figure 3.3 and verify that it can control your S3 and move it to draw shapes just like the simulation. Note: When you are controlling the S3, the **rLocate** statement initializes the robot and it will respond with a beep.

If you want to use the S3 for drawing, consider getting yourself a large white board (Lowes and Home Depot even sell them as 4 foot by 8 foot sheets) and let your S3 draw on it as it moves with a dry erase marker in its center hole. In Figure 3.4, my S3 created a 5-sided polygon on a small whiteboard using the program in Figure 3.3. Note: Since my whiteboard was small, the program in Figure 3.3 only moves the robot 40 units inside the **FOR**-loop. Notice the real robot moved a distance approximately equal to its diameter (which is what the simulator will do for movements of 40 pixels).

Note: *Board Dude* dry erase markers fit the S3 center hole perfectly and can be purchased on Ebay if you have trouble finding them locally. I found they draw much better with a little weight on them to keep the tip pressed to the drawing surface. Figure 3.5 shows a marker with two large nuts on it to provide the weight.

Figure 3.4: A white board makes a great reusable surface for the S3.

Figure 3.5: A little weight on the marker makes it draw much better.

Chapter 4
More on Movement

In Chapter 3 we learned how to write programs to move the simulator, and how to modify those programs so they could control the S3 robot. This chapter will create a program that allows you to remotely control the S3 using your PC's mouse. As in Chapter 3, we will develop the program first on the simulator.

Basic Idea

The basic idea for this program is to create a control panel, on your computer screen, like the one shown in Figure 4.1. Observe that the panel is made up of three parts. Moving the mouse cursor over the center area should move the robot forward. The center area is pointed going forward to make it a little intuitive that this area moves the robot ahead.

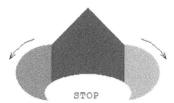

Figure 4.1: Placing the mouse over different areas of this diagram will move the robot.

The areas on either side of the *forward* area of Figure 4.1 are used to rotate the robot either left or right. The curved areas and the arrows hope to make the function of these areas intuitive as well. Pulling the mouse pointer into the stop area below the main diagram should stop the robot. Actually, *any* position that does not rotate or move the robot forward will stop it. The three areas, from left to right, are **Red**, **Blue**, and **LightRed**, even though they show as shades of gray in the print version of this book.

The Program

The program in Figure 4.2 does everything necessary for controlling the simulated robot from the control panel shown in Figure 4.1. This program is larger than previous programs, so now is a good time to learn more about organizing a program.

If you look at the Figure, you will see the statements are combined in smaller groups or modules with a title line (ending in a semicolon) and a terminating line that is either **END** or **RETURN**. All the statements between the title and the terminating line are indented just like we did with loops. Just as with loops, the indenting is not required, but it does make the program easier to read because it helps you see where each module begins and ends. Subroutines are like employees in a company. You can call on them anytime to perform work for you.

The main Module

The first module (**main**) is different from the other four modules in this program because it ends with **END** instead of **RETURN**. It was named **main** because it is *main* part of the program. That particular name is not a requirement; you could just as easily called it **TheProgramStartsHere**. The only real requirements are that the module names must begin with a letter and not contain any spaces or strange characters. Like variables, the names of modules are case sensitive and cannot be the same as a command or function in the language. The **main** program is kind of like a company boss. It decides what needs to be done, and then calls on workers to actually handle the tasks. The boss does not always need to know *how* the workers accomplish their goals.

You will also notice that some of the lines in the program start with two slashes (//). This lets you add comments to your code because everything after // is ignored by RobotBASIC.

Subroutines

The other four modules in the program of Figure 4.2 are called subroutines. Typically subroutines perform some specific task and it usually makes sense to have the name of the subroutine describe the task. The four subroutines in this program are named **InitializeRobot**, **DrawControls**, **DrawObstacles**, and **ControlRobot**. As you would expect, these four subroutines initialize the robot, draw the control panel shown in Figure 4.1, draw some obstacles that the robot must avoid when you drive it around the screen, and allow you to control the robot's movements. In general, the **main** program makes use of subroutines (and often other code too) to simplify how it accomplishes its goals.

Circles and Rectangles

This program draws a lot of circles and rectangles. Both commands require four parameters. The first two parameters define the upper-left corner of a rectangle. The last two parameters define the lower right corner. These two points specify where **Rectangle** will draw its shape. The **Circle** command draws a circle (or ellipse) inside the rectangle defined by the same parameters.

The main Program

The first line in **main** is **gosub DrawControls**. The **gosub** statement tells the computer to GO to the subroutine whose name follows the **gosub** command. That module will be executed until a **return** statement is encountered, which makes the computer return to the line following the **gosub** statement. The important point is that that the use of subroutines breaks a program into smaller functional chunks that make it easier to understand (and to write).

The next two lines in **main** call other subroutines to draw obstacles and initialize the robot. The final line calls the routine that actually allows you to use the mouse to control the robot. Just looking at the **main** program lets you quickly see all the things that the program is doing.

You can then look at each of the subroutines individually and study their code to see how they accomplish their task.

```
main:
   gosub DrawControls
   gosub DrawObstacles
   gosub InitializeRobot
   gosub ControlRobot
end

DrawControls:
   circle 300,500,400,575,RED,RED
   circle 400,500,500,575,LightRED,LightRED
   rectangle 350,500,450,575,BLUE,BLUE
   circle 340,540,460,590,WHITE,WHITE
   xyString 380,560,"STOP"
   // draw triangle
   SetColor BLUE
   Line 350,500,400,450
   LineTo 450,500
   // and fill it with BLUE
   FloodFill2 400,475,BLUE
   SetColor BLACK
   //draw rotate left arrow
   Line 325,492,312,497
   LineTo 298,509
   LineTo 291,519
   LineTo 294,509
   Line 291,519,300,512
   // draw rotate right arrow
   Line 475,492,488,497
   LineTo 502,509
   LineTo 509,519
   LineTo 506,509
   Line 509,519,500,512
return

DrawObstacles:
   LineWidth 3
   Circle 600,200,700,400,BLACK,GREEN
   Rectangle 150,200,400,300,BLACK,GREEN
return
```

```
InitializeRobot:
  rLocate 400,400
  rSpeed 10
return

ControlRobot:
  while TRUE
    ReadMouse x,y,b
    c = PixelClr (x,y)
    if c = BLUE
      rForward 1
    elseif c = RED
      rTurn -1
    elseif c = LightRed
      rTurn 1
    endif
  wend
return
```

Figure 4.2: This program allows manual control of the simulated robot.

A major advantage of organizing a program this way is that it is much easier to understand because it is composed of small modules, each with their own function. Sometime you won't care *how* a module works as long as you know *what* it does for you. The **DrawControls** module is a good example. As mentioned earlier, it creates the image shown in Figure 4.1. And, while you might *want* to examine the code inside this module to see how *it* works, you don't really *need* to do that to understand the general principles of how the entire program works. To prove that point, just ignore the **DrawControls** subroutine for now and turn your attention to the **ControlRobot** module. Remember, it is responsible for letting you use the mouse to control the robot.

Controlling the Robot
Everything inside the **ControlRobot** module is inside a **WHILE** loop, which repeats everything inside the loop as long as the expression following the **WHILE** is true. In this case, the expression is always TRUE, so the loop repeats forever (unless you stop the program).

The loop starts by using a special command called **ReadMouse**. This command obtains information about the mouse and places it into the three variable in the statement. In this case, the variables are **x**, **y**, and **b**, but they could be any three variables. When **ReadMouse** executes, it places the horizontal position of the mouse into the first variable and the vertical position into the second variable. The third variable will contain information about which mouse button is pressed, but we won't need that for this program (even though we have to obtain it).

The next line uses the function **PixelClr** to find the color of the pixel located at screen position **x,y** and store that color in the variable **c**. Since **ReadMouse** stored the mouse position in **x,y**, the variable **c** will contain the color of the screen where the mouse is currently pointing. If that color is **Red**, **Blue**, or **LightRed**, we know the mouse is over the control panel shown in Figure 4.1. As mentioned earlier, these are the colors of the three areas in the panel, from left to right.

This means that if the color is **Blue** we want to move the robot forward and turn it left or right if the color is **Red** or **LightRed**. An **IF** control structure is used to make this happen. Before we look at the code in this module, let's examine **IF** statements.

IF Decisions

RobotBASIC has several types of **IF** statements that can be used to make decisions in your programs. The simplest of these is the **IF-THEN** construct as shown the example below.

```
if x=3 then print x
```

In this example, the **IF** checks to see if the value of **x** is equal to 3. If it is, it performs the action following the **THEN**, which in this case is to print the value of **x**. If **x** is *not* equal to 3 (that is to say, the statement is false), the program just skips the rest of the line and continues on to the next line in the program. This works well when you only have one action that should be performed when the **IF** is true. When you have multiple actions, you need an **IF-ENDIF** as shown below.

```
if y<x
   c = x
   print x
endif
```

In this example, if the value of **y** is less than the value of **x**, then all the statements between the **IF** and the **ENDIF** are executed. If **y** is not less than **x** (**y** is greater than or equal to **x**) then execution will continue with the line following the **ENDIF**. If you want to do something different when the **IF** is false, then you can use an **IF-ELSE-ENDIF** as shown below.

```
if a<12
   a = 12
else
   a = a+1
   print a
endif
```

In this example, when the **IF** is true, everything between the **IF** and the **ELSE** will be executed. Otherwise, everything between the **ELSE** and the **ENDIF** is executed. In either case, execution will continue with the line following the **ENDIF**. Finally, if we have multiple decisions deciding what should be done, we can use and **IF-ELSEIF-ELSE-ENDIF** structure as shown below.

```
if (x+y) <= 36
   print "the sum is less than or equal to 36"
elseif x = 36
   print "the value of x is 36"
elseif y < 0
   print "the value of y is negative"
else
   print "none of the others were true"
endif
```

This form of the **IF** is the most versatile. Each **elseif** section can check for a different condition and can have multiple statements to execute. Once a true decision is found, its section executes and the program continues with the first statement after the **ENDIF**. The **ELSE** block is optional.

This **ELSEIF** version of the **IF** is used in the **ControlRobot** subroutine in Figure 4.2. It makes the simulated robot move forward when the mouse is over the **BLUE** middle section of the control panel and turn left or right when it is over the **Red** and **LightRed** sections.

It is important to realize that even though this is a relatively large program (for beginners) the modular design makes it easy to understand. The **ControlRobot** module, as we have just seen, is easy to follow, even with many new commands. Remember, you can always use the RobotBASIC HELP file to get more information on any command. Just click the **?** in the menu bar at the top of the RobotBASIC editor screen.

Remember that you don't really have to understand the details of every module in the program in order to understand the overall operation of the program. You know, for example, that the **DrawControls** module draws the control panel, but unless you want to modify the code, it is not really essential that you know how every line of code in that module works. Even so, many readers will want to learn more about graphics. Both the **DrawObstacles** and the **InitializeRobot** modules are small and easy to understand so let's focus on **DrawControls**.

Drawing the Control Panel
The subroutine in Figure 4.2 draws the control panel shown in Figure 4.1. A more sophisticated drawing could have been made with less code, but for beginners, it is important to keep things as simple as possible. For that reason, most of the drawing is created with overlapping circles and rectangles. The first two lines in **DrawControls** create two circles as shown in Figure 4.3, Part A.

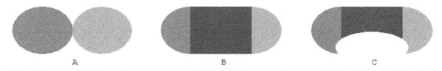

Figure 4.3: These drawings show how overlapping objects help create the control panel.

The next line draws a rectangle that overlaps the two circles as shown in Part B of Figure 4.3. Next, a white circle is drawn as shown in Part C. This creates the bottom portion of the panel. The program then uses Line statements to draw a triangle as shown in Figure 4.4, Part A. Then a **FloodFill2** command is used to fill the area inside the triangle with blue. Finally, the word STOP is printed as shown in Part C with an **xyString** command. The **xyString** is very similar to print, but it allows you to specify the x,y coordinates of *where* to print.

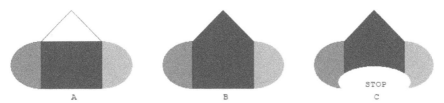

Figure 4.4: These steps almost complete the control panel.

The only thing left is to draw the arrows (see Figure 4.1). This is done with a series of line statements. RobotBASIC has many graphic commands that make it easy to draw interesting things. And don't forget, if you want to learn more about any of the new programming statements used throughout this book, just look in the HELP file.

Controlling the Simulation
When you have the program entered and free of errors, run it, and use the mouse to control the simulated robot. Move the mouse pointer over appropriate areas on the control panel to move the robot forward or to make it rotate left or right. Since the robot rotates when it turns, the path it takes is straight and angular as shown in Figure 4.5. There are no safeguards (we will save that for a later chapter) so it is easy to drive the robot into a wall or obstacle, causing the program to terminate with an error. Such problems will be addressed in Chapter 5.

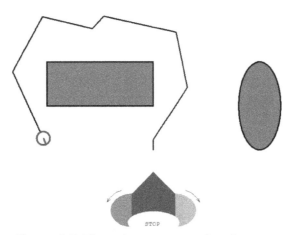

Figure 4.5: The robot rotates when it turns.

Turning Instead of Rotating

The fact that the robot rotates instead of turning is not a bad thing as it makes the robot very maneuverable in tight spots. It is easy to modify the way the robot handles turning though. Add an **rForward 1** statement after each of the **rTurn** statements in Figure 4.2 and run the program to see how the robot handles turns. The path your robot takes should be more similar to that shown in Figure 4.6. Of course, your robot will not leave a trail unless you add an **rPen DOWN** to your program and you will need an **rInvisible** command if you want to be able to drive over the line.

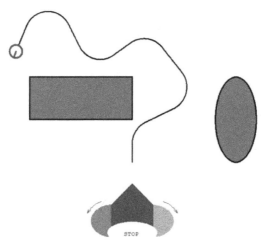

Figure 4.6: This style of turns may be preferred by some.

Controlling How Fast the Robot Turns

You can make the robot turn *slower* by adding another **rForward 1** statement immediately after each **rForward 1** that we added earlier. You can make the robot turn *faster* by having additional **rTurn 1** statements for each **rForward**. Experiment with these changes and watch how the simulator reacts. Can you explain how the modifications change the robot behavior?

Controlling the S3

Now that we have a program that allows you to control the simulated robot using your mouse, we need to modify the program so it can control the S3 robot. Before using the S3 though, convert the program back to its origin state (remove the extra **rForward** statements we added to modify how the robot turns). In order to control the real robot, we just need to set up the proper Bluetooth channel before executing the **rLocate** statement (just as we did in Chapter 3). This can be done many ways, but it is suggested that you place the following line at the beginning of your program (use your port number), and then modify the **InitializeRobot** module as shown in Figure 4.7.

```
PortNum = 5
```

If you look carefully at figure 4.7, you will notice two differences from previous conversions. One such difference is a new statement, **rCommand(1,100)**. We will discuss this new instruction shortly, but for now, just accept that it is necessary to make the S3 respond like the simulated robot. The second change is that an **IF-THEN** statement only executes the **rCommPort** command if **PortNum** is greater than zero. This makes it easy to use the same program to control BOTH the simulator and the S3. Just set **PortNum** to zero if you want to control the simulator and to the port number for your Bluetooth communication if you want to control the S3.

```
InitializeRobot:
  if PortNum>0 then rCommPort PortNum
  rLocate 400,400
  rCommand(1,100)
  rSpeed 10
return
```
Figure 4.7: With minor changes, you can control the real robot with your mouse.

Of course, you don't need many of the things found in the simulator program. For example, you don't need to set the robot's speed (it does not affect the S3) and you certainly don't need to draw obstacles on the screen. It does not hurt to do such things though so type in the simulation program and after you get it working, modify it so you can control the S3 with your mouse. If you don't want some of these things (such as the obstacles) you can easily use the same **PortNum** technique used to prevent execution of **rCommPort**. To eliminate obstacle when controlling the S3, for example, just replace **gosub DrawObstacles** in the **main** routine with **if rCommPort=0 then gosub DrawObstacles**. This will ensure obstacles are only drawn when the simulator is being used.

Driving the Real Robot
Be careful when you control the real robot. As with the simulation, there are no safeguards so you can easily run the robot into walls or objects in the room. Drive the robot carefully, because, unlike the simulation, when the real robot hits something it will not cause an error and stop the program. Chapter 5 will begin our exploration of sensors and how they can be used by the robot to control its own behavior. One of the first things we will do is program the robot help us by refusing to drive into objects even when we tell it to do so.

Before we move on to sensors though, there are a few more things to discuss about the remote control program. If you modify the program of Figure 4.2 so that it can control the S3, you will see that the real robot moves just like the simulation as depicted in Figure 4.5. If you try to add the **rForward** statements to make the S3 move like Figure 4.6, you will see that the S3 responds in a jerky, spastic, manner as it tries to make turns.

Jerky Movement
The reason for the jerky motion is not immediately obvious to most people. In the remote-controlled simulation, the combination of **rTurn** and **rForward** causes the robot to respond in a gentle curve, just as we would expect. Why would this combination of rotation and forward movements work perfectly well with the simulator, but not with a real robot?

In order to see the problem let's just look at a right turn (made up of an **rTurn 1** and an **rForward 1**). During the **rTurn**, the left wheel continues to move forward, but the right wheel is reversed (causing the expected rotation around the robot's center). During the **rForward** motion, both wheels move forward. This means that during a right turn, the right wheel is constantly changing directions, moving forward during the **rForward** period, then moving backward during the **rTurn**. Since a real robot has mass and inertia, this constant changing of directions makes the robot respond with jerky movements.

What we need is a way for the real robot to make turns like these WITHOUT having to reverse the direction of one of its wheel (as the simulator does). The solution while not obvious, is rather simple. Instead of reversing one wheel (producing rotation) we simply need to slow down that wheel, allowing the robot to turn in a gentle curve. We DO NOT want this action all the time though.

As we saw in Chapter 3, when the S3 is making turns like **rTurn 5** or **rTurn 90**, we ALWAYS want it to respond *just like the simulation* (reversing one wheel and rotating around its center). If it did not respond this way, the polygons in Chapter 3 would have rounded corners. We only want the robot to turn by slowing down one wheel when we execute an **rTurn 1** or **rTurn -1** in a loop as we did earlier in this Chapter. Furthermore, it would be nice if we could control how much we reduced the speed of the slow wheel (allowing us to control how fast the robot turns). To make things even more complicated, there will always be situations where we will still want the S3 to use a rotational movement for **rTurn 1** and **rTurn -1**.

A Solution

All this sounds horribly complicated, but the RROSS program makes it easy for the programmer. First of all, the RROSS will *automatically* cause rotational turns whenever you use an **rTurn** statement whose parameter is greater than 1 or less than -1. When you use turns of 1 or -1, the way the *slow* wheel responds is controlled by the special command mentioned earlier, **rCommand(1,100)**. The first parameter (1, in this case) specifies *what* we are trying to do. The 1 is a special code used to indicate we are wanting to change how the S3 reacts to **rTurn 1** and **rTurn -1** statements – we want to change the *turn style* of the robot.

The second parameter in this command (100, in this case) controls how the robot will actually behave for **rTurn 1** and **rTurn -1**. If the second parameter in this command is 100, the S3 will make rotational turns, just like the simulator (which is why we added this command to the **InitializeRobot** module of Figure 4.7). Any number less than 100 will control the speed of the slow wheel (but only during turns with a parameter of 1 or -1). Issuing an **rCommand(1,60)** for example, will make the slow wheel turn at 60% of the fast wheel.

Slowing a wheel in this manner turns the robot gently, but it also moves it forward. This means that an **rTurn** alone can replace the **rTurn-rForward** pair used earlier. If you want to confirm this for yourself, run the program in Figure 4.7 and watch the path taken by the S3. It will be a circle and you can control the radius of the circle by changing the second parameter in the **rCommand** statement. Note: The S3's default turn style for **rTurn**s of 1 and -1 is slow and gentle, not the rotational style of the simulation. As we pursue a variety of projects, you will see that this choice is the best for most situations.

```
rCommPort 5 // use your port number
rLocate 100,100
rCommand(1,50)// change 50 to alter the rate of turn
while TRUE
  rTurn 1
wend
```

Figure 4.7: This example program moves the S3 in a circle (without an **rForward**).

rCommands

The RROSS has many **rCommand**s that allow you to handle special situations by giving the S3 capabilities that the simulator does not have. Future Chapters will introduce **rCommand**s when needed and Appendix A will summarize all of your options. Once you start using **rCommand**s, you will see they are far easier to use than you might.

Chapter 5
Sensor Controlled Movement

It could be argued that the robot discussed in previous chapters is not *really* a robot. The definition of a robot can be different depending on who you ask, but a definition that I like is:

> **Robot**: A mechanical device that can react appropriately to changes in its environment while performing tasks without human intervention.

The key aspect of this definition is that the robot can, on its own, change its behavior when it encounters different situations. This is far different from a remote control toy or even a complex machine such as a car. Think about a car for a moment.

The car responds to your requests. When you push the gas pedal, the motor speeds up and when you press the brake the car slows or stops, but *you* are making the decisions about what to do and when to do it. There are some aspects of a car that are a little *robotic*. If you set the cruise control to 50 mph, for example, the car will attempt (on its own) to maintain that speed, even if it encounters changes in its environment such as a steep hill.

A typical car, however, will not react appropriately if another car pulls in front of it and slows down. Instead of slowing down, most cars with cruise control will just continue to maintain their speed. So maybe, we can consider a car's cruise control to be a bit robotic in nature, but if it could also react appropriately to cars pulling front of it (by slowing down to avoid a collision) then it would certainly be more robotic. In the near future, most cars will probably have more robotic capabilities. This discussion simply implies that some robots are more intelligent that other robots. An ideal robot should be able to react, not just to changes in its environment, but to *unexpected* changes.

Robot programmers try to *predict* all the situations their robots might *normally* encounter. Often robot builders try to limit their robot's environment so that unexpected situations do not occur. Robots that help with building things in a manufacturing plant are a good example. In many cases, the area around such robots is fenced off so that nothing can enter their environment and create unexpected situations that might cause problems. Most human deaths involving manufacturing robots were due (at least in part) by humans improperly entering a robot's space and creating a situation the robot was not programmed to handle.

Machine Intelligence

If a robot can react to *new and unique* situations, we say it is intelligent. Often we call it artificial intelligence (AI) to distinguish it from human intelligence, but some people, including myself, prefer the term *machine intelligence*. Many companies are trying to add AI to cars and it appears that their efforts are very successful. In the near future it is not unreasonable to expect that most cars will be able to drive themselves and handle new and unique situations in order to prevent accidents, avoid traffic jams, and much, much more.

Robots and AI will play a big part in the future and the more knowledge you have of such subjects, the better prepared you will be for the job market. Much of the remainder of this book is devoted to helping you understand how robots can react appropriately to changes in their environment. Obviously we are not going to be able to make the S3 super intelligent, but we will be able to make it handle a variety of tasks on its own.

Senses

No robot can interact with its environment, unless it can somehow *observe* its environment. Humans do this with senses of sight, touch, etc. If you had no senses, you would not have any idea of what was going on around you. The same is true of a robot. If we want it to react to environmental changes that it might encounter, we need to give it senses.

The S3 has the ability to sense when an object is in front of it. It does this by shining an infrared (IR) light (invisible to humans) forward from two LEDs (one at a time). If this light hits a nearby object and is reflective back, it can be detected with a special light sensitive transistor (front center of the S3) as shown in Figure 5.1.

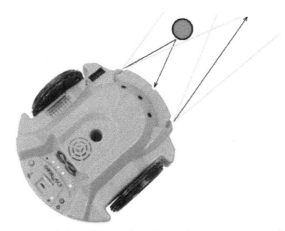

Figure 5.1: IR light allows the S3 to detect nearby objects.

In the Figure, the left-side LED is emitting light that is reflected off the object back to the detecting transistor indicating that an object is detected left of center. The right beam is not reflected back, so it does not "see" an object. Since the computer inside the S3 turns on the left and right IR LEDs individually it can determine if the object is seen by the left or the right beam and thus determine if the object is slightly left or right of center. If both beams see the object, we assume the object is directly in front of the S3 (even though it could be two objects).

The Simulator's Perimeter Sensors
Figure 5.2 shows the five *feel* sensors on the simulator. Most real robot used by students and hobbyists do not have so many, but having five lets the simulator replicate the sensory capability for a variety of robots. Notice the simulators sensors are labeled 1, 2, 4, 8, and 16. The reason for these numbers will be discussed later in this book.

Figure 5.2: The simulator has five perimeter proximity sensors.

We will use the sensors labeled 2, 4, and 8 for use with the S3 because they are *most closely aligned* with the S3's sensors, although the S3 sensors are both pointing more forward as shown in Figure 5.1. Look at Figure 5.2 when you read the following. Remember, if both of the S3 IR sensors detect objects, we assume the object is directly in front of the S3. For that reason, when both of the S3's sensors detect an object, the RROSS software inside the S3 will activate the simulator's sensor 4 (because it points directly forward). If the S3's left IR sensor alone sees an object, the RROSS will activate sensor 8. Similarly, if only the right IR sensor sees an object, sensor 2 will be activated.

The rFeel() Function
In order to demonstrate how this works with the real robot we will use the short program in Figure 5.3. When you run the program it will initialize the S3 and enter the **while**-loop. The first statement inside the loop tells the S3 to move forward a zero amount. While this appears to do nothing, it is *required* for this program to work. The RROSS program sends important, time sensitive, sensory data back to RobotBASIC every time RobotBASIC requests the S3 to move in any way. This methodology makes the communication with the S3 faster, because RobotBASIC never really has to request the main sensor data. It just gets returned automatically every time the robot is told to move. In this situation we don't really want the robot moving, but telling it to move forward a zero amount will automatically update the sensor data inside of RobotBASIC.

RobotBASIC allows you to access the sensor data represented in Figure 5.2 using the function **rFeel()**. Functions have a value just like a variable or number and you can use them in the same ways you would any number or variable. In the program of Figure 5.3, an **xyString** command prints the value of the feel sensors. (Remember, **xyString** is very much like **PRINT**, except that it allows you to control where things are printed.) Since these actions are inside the endless loop, the value of the sensors will be print over and over in the upper-left corner of the screen (position 10,10).

```
rCommPort 5 // use your port number
rLocate 400,300
while true
  rForward 0
  xyString 10,10,rFeel()
wend
```

Figure 5.3: This program lets you test the S3's IR sensors.

If you run this program, the S3 will beep once when it is initialized with the **rLocate** statement, and then remain motionless. The number being printed on the screen should be a 0, 2, 4 or 8, depending on which of the S3 sensors detect an object within its range (0 means nothing is seen). Place your hand directly in front of the S3 and about one foot away from the robot. Slowly move your hand toward the robot while watching the screen. When you get close enough (perhaps within 6 to 8 inches) you should see the 0 on the screen turn into a 4 (indicating something is directly in front of the robot).

Once you get a number other than zero, move your hand slowly left and right and you should see the number on the screen vary among the possible options (0, 2, 4, and 8) indicating whether your hand is directly in front (4) or left (8) or right (2) or not close enough or too far left or right to be seen (0). With the S3's IR sensors, you do not have to move your hand much from side-to-side to get all of these numbers (because the IR beams point pretty much forward). We will expand the S3's capabilities in Chapter 9 and create a much more sophisticated perimeter sensing system. For now though, the S3's built in IR sensors will do fine.

Don't worry if some of the above discussion seems complicated. Once you see the IR sensors in action, you will discover they are very easy to use.

Reacting to Objects

Let's use the simulator to develop some programs that use the **rFeel()** sensors. Once you understand how they work, you can use them with the S3. Look at the short program in Figure 5.4. After the simulated robot is initialized in the center of the screen, a **while**-loop moves the robot forward as long as none of the **rFeel()** sensors are on. Notice how the reserved word **NOT** is used to reverse the TRUE or FALSE condition of the statement. (**rFeel()** is TRUE if ANY of the sensors are on.) The **while** statement could also have been written as **while rFeel()=0**. Both indicate that none of the sensors are seeing an obstacle.

```
rLocate 400,300
while not rFeel()
  rForward 1
wend
```

Figure 5.4: This program moves the robot until it reaches an object.

This means the loop in Figure 5.4 makes the simulated robot move when it does not see an object, but further investigation can show the simulator is not acting as much like the S3 as we want. Look at Figure 5.5 to see what happens to the robot's movement when an object is drawn on the screen near the robot's path.

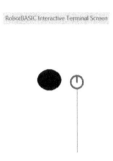

Figure 5.5: The robot stopped because of the simulator's side sensor.

If you remember putting your hand in front of the S3's sensors, you know that its IR sensors really only detect objects that are in front of the robot. Anything off to the side is simply not seen. Since the simulator has five sensors (Figure 5.2) it can see off to the side as well as forward. That can be nice, but it can be confusing if we are developing programs that will eventually run on the S3. We need a way to ignore the simulator's two side sensors. An easy way to do this is to replace the **while** statement in Figure 5.5 with the one below. Note that the entire expression is in parenthesis because we want the **&** operation to be performed before the **NOT** operation.

```
while not (rFeel()&14)
```

The **&** operator allows us to use a number (14 in this case) to control which sensors we want to use. The number 14 was chosen because it is the sum of 8, 4, and 2, which are the sensors (see Figure 5.2) that we want to use (we want the robot to move forward when none of these three, and only these three, sensors see an object). If we rerun the program with this change, the output will be like Figure 5.6 which shows that the robot moves right past the obstacle because it did not see it. As expected, it still stops when it sees the top of the window with its forward facing sensors. The top of the screen is seen as a wall.

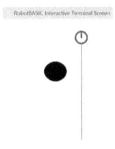

Figure 5.6: The simulated robot now cannot see to its side.

The program in Figure 5.4 simply stops when it encounters an object. We could have it rotate 180^0 move away, but we can make it better than that. Since the value of **rFeel()** also tells us if the object is slightly on the left or on the right, we can use that information to turn the robot in the opposite direction. Look at the program in Figure 5.7. It makes the robot behave differently depending on which sensor sees an object. Notice that the **&** is again used to specify which sensor we want to check. If the left sensor (8) is on, we turn left 45^0, if the right sensor (2) is on, we turn right 45^0, and if the middle sensor (4) is on we turn 180^0. If no sensors are triggered (the **ELSE** condition) the robot simply moves forward.

These examples show how the **&** operator can allow you to only look at one or more sensors. To fully understand how this works, you need some knowledge of binary math and binary operators (the **&** performs a binary **AND** operation). The good news is that even if you have not studied those subjects in school, you can still specify which sensor or sensors you want to check or use by just mimicking these examples. This is a great example of why the study of mathematics can be very helpful when programming a robot.

```
circle 300,100,360,150,BLACK,BLACK
rLocate 400,300
rInvisible GREEN
rPen Down
while TRUE
  if (rFeel()&8)
    rTurn 45
  elseif (rFeel()&2)
    rTurn -45
  elseif (rFeel()&4)
    rTurn 180
  else
    rForward 1
  endif
wend
```

Figure 5.7: This program lets the robot roam around the screen.

If you just look at the program you might think it should work fine. Unfortunately, if you run the program, the robot just moves back and forth between the top and bottom walls. Try it and see for yourself. It does this because the robot is initially facing the top wall, so it sees the top wall with the middle sensor (turns 180^0), then sees the lower wall and does the same thing – and this just continues *forever*. Very boring.

We can improve on this behavior by making the robot turn a random amount when it see something with the middle sensor. This can be done by replacing the **rTurn 180** statement with **rTurn 150+random(60)**. The **random(60)** function will produce a random number between 0 and 60 and when that is added to 150 will produce a number between 150 and 210. Make this change and rerun the program. You should see the output shown in Figure 5.8. Run your program and watch the robot roam around the screen.

When you have your program working, modify it so instead of it making 45° turns, it makes random turns between 35 and 55 (and between -35 and-55). When you get everything working, the program's output should be fairly random as shown in Figure 5.9. Try adding some more objects to the robot's environment. Verify that it can avoid them too.

RobotBASIC Interactive Terminal Screen [NoName.BAS]

Figure 5.8: The robot now turns away from the wall at a random angle.

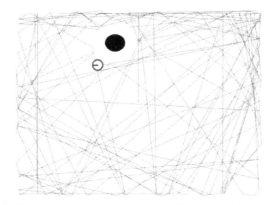

Figure 5.9: The robot roams randomly while avoiding objects.

Roaming with the S3

With all the previous examples to guide you, you should be able to modify the simulator roaming program to make it work with the S3. Make the needed modifications and try it out to verify that it works as expected. The S3 should respond similarly to the simulation, but not quite. Keep in mind that the 8-4-2 sensors on the simulator are spaced 45° apart while the S3's sensors are much more forward in their orientation. This makes it even more unlikely for the S3 (compared to the simulated robot) to see objects off to the side.

Improving the Remote Control

If you recall from Chapter 4, you could easily crash either the simulator or the S3 by driving it into an obstacle. Now that you know how to use the perimeter sensors, we can improve the robot's remote control behavior. Refer back to Figure 4.2 in Chapter 4. When you told the robot to move forward, the program just executed an **rForward 1** statement. If we replace that statement with the following line: **if not (rFeel()&14) then rForward 1**, the robot will *refuse* to move forward if it sees an object in its way. It will still turn left and right, so you can rotate the robot until there is a clear area in front of it so it will move forward for you. Make these changes and verify that the robot (either the simulation or the S3) will not let you run into objects. Remember though, that the simulation and especially the S3 cannot see to the side so some collisions might still be possible. In later chapters we will improve on the S3's sensory capabilities and thus allow it perform better in many situations.

Producing Sounds for Feedback

The S3 has the ability to produce tones and the RROSS makes it easy to produce simple tones with programming statements. We can use tones to provide feedback to us for specific situations. In this situation, it could be nice if the S3 were to beep when it was stuck in a situation where you were telling it to move forward and it was refusing. You could do this by replacing the original **rForward** statement (as discussed above) with the code in Figure 5.10.

```
if not(rFeel()&14)
   rForward 1
else
  rCommand(11, 100)
  delay 500
endif
```

Figure 5.10: This code can make the remote-controlled S3 beep when it is blocked.

Figure 5.10 shows another **rCommand**. In this case, the command code is 11. This tells the S3 we want it to make a sound that is ½ second in duration. The second parameter is used to specify a frequency (the actual frequency produced is 10 times the parameter).   There are other **rCommands** can be used to control the duration of the tone and the frequency multiplier, but this one command is enough for now.

The **delay** command in Figure 5.10 makes the robot pause 500ms (½ second) between beeps. Make these changes to the remote control program from Chapter 4 and verify that your S3 will beep when you try to drive it into an obstacle. Experiment with different frequencies and find one that you like. You might even try a low frequency then higher frequency with no delays. Since this pattern will repeat when the robot is blocked it will make a unique sound. Try it.

Chapter 6
Finding a Light

Now that sensors have been introduced, let's write a program that demonstrates how to use the S3's light sensors. There are three phototransistors mounted on the front of the S3 as shown in Figure 6.1. Each of these sensors can determine the brightness of the light that strikes them. Our first project for this Chapter is to program the robot to face the brightest light in the room, which could be a window or even a flashlight in a dimly lit room.

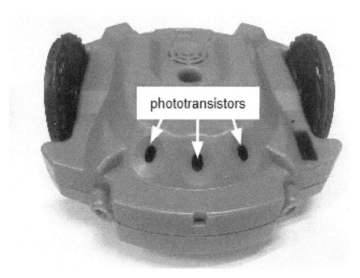

Figure 6.1: There are three light sensors on the front of the S3.

Creating a Simulation

RobotBASIC's simulated robot does not have light sensors, so we cannot use the simulation to *directly* develop programs that involve sensing light. The RROSS system however makes use of two simulator functions that are not for sensing light, **rLook()** and **rBumper()**. The RROSS has been designed so that both of these functions can be used to access the S3's light sensors (but each in a different way). With a little creativity, we can create a simulation that will at least help us test the basic principles of searching for the brightest light.

The rLook() Function

The **rLook()** function is normally used on the simulator as a simple camera, enabling the simulated robot to look for objects of a specified color. If you use **c = rLook(0)** for example, it will look directly ahead of the robot and assign the first non-invisible color seen to the variable **c**. The zero parameter is specifying to look directly forward.

Look at the program in Figure 6.2. The main program draws a green circle on the screen to represent a bright light. After the robot is initialized, the **FaceLight** module is called to find the *light*. We want **FaceLight** to rotate the robot through 360⁰ in 15⁰ increments and update the variable **Angle** with the angle the robot is currently facing when it sees **GREEN**. This angle, of course, is relative to the robot's starting position. Notice how the variable **i** in the **FOR**-loop keeps track of the angle the robot is currently facing. This is definitely different from looking for the brightest light (it always looks for a *green light*), but it lets us build a similar program to get started. Once it is working, and you understand it, it can be easily modified to meet our real goal of making the S3 look for the brightest light.

```
main:
   circle 50,300,110,360,GREEN,GREEN
   gosub InitRobot
   gosub FaceLight
end

InitRobot:
   rLocate 400,300
return

FaceLight:
   Angle=0
   for i= 0 to 345 step 15
     c = rLook(0)
     if c=GREEN
        Angle=i
     endif
     rTurn 15
   next
   if Angle<=180
     rTurn Angle
   else
     rTurn Angle-360
   endif
return
```

Figure 6.2: This program turns the robot to face a green circle.

When the loop is complete, the variable **Angle** contains the angle to the brightest light (relative to the starting point, which is also the ending point since the robot rotates a total of 360 degrees – can you explain how the robot turns a total of 360⁰?). This makes it easy to turn to that angle. We could just turn the robot **Angle** degrees, but if **Angle** is greater than 180, it makes more sense to turn the robot left **360-a** degrees (can you explain why this makes more sense?). This is done inside an **IF-ELSE** structure. Using a parameter of **Angle-360** creates a negative number to force a left turn.

Type in this program and test it to see that it works as expected. Try moving the circle to different places on the screen to verify the program can always find it. What would happen if you placed two circles on the screen? Which one would it find? Can you explain why?

Using the S3

When using **rLook()** with the S3, it returns a number indicating how bright the light is on a specified sensor (bigger numbers implies a brighter light. If you use **rLook()** alone or **rLook(0)**, the reading will be for the center sensor (0 degrees). If you use any negative parameter the reading will be for the left sensor and positive numbers greater than zero will be used for the right sensor.

The program in Figure 6.3 is a modified version of Figure 6.2 that will make the S3 find the brightest light in the room. The areas of the program that involve changes have been highlighted with **BOLD** text. Notice that now there are two variables keeping track of what is happening as the robot rotates and takes readings.

```
main:
  PortNum = 5 // use your port number
  gosub InitRobot
  gosub FaceLight
end

InitRobot:
  rCommPort PortNum
  rLocate 400,300
return

FaceLight:
  Angle=0
  Light = 0
  for i= 0 to 345 step 15
    c = rLook()
    if c>Light
      Light = c
      Angle = i
    endif
    rTurn 15
  next
  if a<=180
    rTurn a
  else
    rTurn a-360
  endif
return
```

Figure 6.3: This program points the robot towards the brightest light in the room.

The variable **Angle** still keeps track of where we see the light, but in this program we only want to record angles *when the light is brighter than previous readings*. We do this by setting the variable **Light** to zero (the smallest possible number), and then updating its value whenever we see a light brighter than the last highest value. Of course, when this happens (a brighter light is seen), we also need to update the value of **Angle** to reflect the current direction.

In summary, the commands for the simulated robot were not exactly what we needed, but they was close enough to permit developing a similar program to what we wanted. While not perfect, at least this lets you do a lot of the work at home (where you might not have a robot if you are a student). It also lets you get the basic principles of the program working on a simulator version that can be modified for use with the S3. This extremely valuable, because, as you will see, getting the simulator to perform properly is often much easier than working with the real robot. This is true because you can precisely control the simulated robot's environment and the simulated robot does not damage things it crashes into.

Reusable Code
One of the nice things about isolating the code used to find the brightest light into the **FindLight** subroutine is that you can easily copy and paste the module into a new program if you needed this behavior for a future project. Since you know the module is fully debugged and working, using it in future programs can greatly reduce development time.

Testing the Program
You can perform a simple test by just sitting the S3 in the center of a room and run the program. The robot should rotate 360° and then turn to face the brightest spot in the room, which will probably be a window or lamp. If the room is relatively dark, you could place a flashlight on the floor a few feet away from the robot and pointing directly toward it. After running the program, the robot should be facing the light (within a 15° margin of error because the robot only measured the light every 15°).

Tracking Toward a Light
The simulator has an **rBumper()** function that is not used for the basic S3 (it will be used for the enhanced S3 in Chapter 9), so the RROSS can use it to report additional light sensor data when the S3 is in its default standard mode. Inside the RROSS program, the light intensity of the three light sensors (Figure 6.1) is compared. If they are all relatively *close* to the same value, the RROSS will make the value of **rBumper()** equal to zero. If the right sensor detects the brightest light, the value set will be 2. If the center sensor is brightest, the value will be 4, and if the left sensor is brightest, the value will be 8. Notice these numbers correspond with the same positions used by **rFeel()** so everything is consistent.

Of course, you could calculate which sensor is detecting the brightest light by making three **rLook()** readings, but **rBumper()** does all the work for you and is much faster than the communication needed to take multiple readings. Keep in mind that the **rBumper()** data on the simulator has no similarity to the light sensor information on the S3. We are only using the

rBumper() function as an easy and efficient way to obtain the light information from the S3. For this reason, the simulator cannot *directly* help in developing our next program.

For our next program, we want to use the **rBumper()** data to control the S3 in much the same way that we did with the remote control panel in Chapter 4. Since the remote control program is similar to what we want to do in this chapter, and since it was developed with the simulator, we can still give a little credit to the simulation for developing the principles we will use to build a light tracking program.

Our goal is for the finished program to move the robot toward a light by turning left or right depending on which light sensors is seeing the brightest light. This would allow you to shine a flashlight on the robot to control it (similar to using the mouse in Chapter 4) or, if you had a bright light on your back, the robot could follow you as you move about.

Figure 6.4 shows how easy it is to create such a program. You should feel comfortable with most of the program so all we will look at is the new **FollowLight** subroutine. A **while**-loop ensures at the robot will continue trying to get to the light as long as no objects are blocking its path. This is done by checking the state of the *feel* sensors (to prevent collisions).

Inside the loop, three **IF**-statements check for each of the possible **rBumper()** conditions. If the sensor state is 0 or 4, meaning none of the sensors are brighter or the center sensor is brighter, the robot is commanded to move forward. If the left sensor is brightest (8) the robot turns to the left and if the right sensor is brightest, the robot right. Notice the similarity of this code to the remote control program in Chapter 4.

Remember, the default style of the S3 turns is slow and gentle but you can modify that to your liking with an **rCommand** as discussed in Chapter 4.

```
main:
  PortNum = 5 // use your port number
  gosub InitRobot
  gosub FollowLight
end

InitRobot:
  rCommPort PortNum
  rLocate 100,100
return

FollowLight:
  while  not rFeel()
    if rBumper()=4 or rbumper()=0 then rforward 1
    if rBumper()=2 then rTurn 1
    if rBumper()=8 then rTurn -1
  wend
return
```

Figure 6.4: This program makes the robot follow a moving light.

Testing Light Tracking with the S3

Test the program by moving around with a bright light (perhaps a lamp without a shade or a flashlight pointed at the S3's sensors). As you move to the side, the robot should turn toward the light and move toward it when pointed toward it. This tracking behavior should continue until the robot gets to the light or is blocked by some other obstacle that triggers its **rFeel()** sensors.

Debugging Your Programs

The programs in this chapter are fairly small, so this is a good time to discuss finding errors in your code or logic. For our initial example, load the program of Figure 6.2 into RobotBASIC. Insert the command **Stepping ON** as the first line in the **FaceLight** module. When you run the program, everything will execute at full speed until the **Stepping ON** command is encountered. At that point, a debug window will appear. You should resize the debug window as necessary and arrange the edit and output windows so you can see everything as shown in Figure 6.5. Notice that the line following the **Stepping On** is highlighted in the editor. Notice also that the debug screen is indicating that the same line is about to be executed.

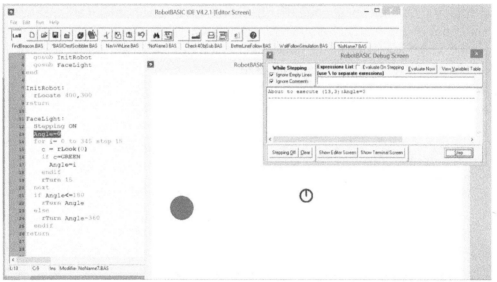

Figure 6.5: Arrange the edit, output, and debug windows so you can see everything.

Click the STEP button in the DEBUG window and watch the actions in both the editor and the debug screen. With each click, the program will execute the next statement. Keep clicking and watch it move through the **FOR**-loop. Watch the output screen every time the **rTurn 15** instruction is executed. You will see the robot rotating as each pass through the loop executes.

Keep stepping until you have executed the **c = rLook(0)** command. This means the value read by the front light sensor should be stored in the variable **c**. You can use the debug window to evaluate the variable **c** as shown in Figure 6.6. Just type **c** into the space at the top of the window (see the Figure) and click **Evaluate Now**. You will see that **c** has a current value of **-1** (see Figure 6.6).

Figure 6.6: You can check the value of variables and expressions.

Since it does not see any colors in the direction the robot is pointing, **rLook(0)** returned a value of **-1**. It can't use **0** because that is the number used internally for the color **BLACK**. Keep stepping through the program and notice the **IF**-statement inside the loop is never true, so the line inside the **IF** is not executed. Keep stepping through the loop until the robot is facing the green circle (this can take a while, if you want something faster, modify the program so the ball is on the other side of the screen and start over).

When the robot is pointing at the circle and you have executed the line **c = rLook(0)**, use the debug window to check the value of **c** again. This time, you should see that it equals 3 which is the value RobotBASIC uses for **GREEN**. Figure 6.7 shows the list of standard colors used in RobotBASIC and the values used to represent them.

•Color Constants

•Black	= 0
•Blue	= 1
•Green	= 2
•Cyan	= 3
•Red	= 4
•Magenta	= 5
•Brown	= 6
•Gray	= 7
•Darkgray	= 8
•Lightblue	= 9
•Lightgreen	=10
•Lightcyan	=11
•Lightred	=12
•Lightmagenta	=13
•Yellow	=14
•White	=15

Figure 6.7: This information was cut-and-pasted from the RobotBASIC HELP screen.

Continue stepping through the program and notice that this time, the **IF** is true, so **Angle** will be set equal to the current angle which is stored in the variable **i**. If you want to try more examples, create several circles on the screen of different colors and watch what number is read by **rLook()** for each circle.

If you only want to check the value of **c** in the program as it runs, there are ways to speed things up. Just place the **Stepping ON** command directly after the **c = rLook(0)** statement. This will make the program stop at just the right place to evaluate the value of **c**. You can then step a few times or you can just click the **Stepping Off** button. This will let the program run at full speed until it gets to the **Stepping ON** statement again (the next time through the loop).

As you get used to debugging a program, you can sprinkle **Stepping ON** statements throughout your program at places you want to see how the program is reacting. When you are finished with a particular evaluation, just click **Stepping Off** and the program will run at full speed until it gets to your next **Stepping ON** statement.

Try these ideas with one of the programs that controls the S3. You will see the S3 move as you step, and when you evaluate sensor data it will be what is actually read by the sensors on the S3. RobotBASIC has other tools for helping you debug a program, but this is probably all most readers will need. Curious and advanced readers should consult the HELP file.

Chapter 7
Line Sensors: Following a Line

Now that you know how to control the S3's movements with sensor data, let's create a project that does something a little more exciting. The S3 has a variety of sensors that allow that allow it to interact with its environment. We have used the front IR sensors to detect objects in front of the robot. This chapter will concentrate on two other sensors called *line sensors*.

The line sensors can be found on the bottom of the S3 as shown in Figure 7.1. Each sensor is composed of two parts. One is an LED that emits infrared light like the front perimeter sensors (invisible to the human eye). The second part is a photo transistor that can detect the IR light when it is reflected off a surface such as the floor. This gives the S3 the ability to determine when its sensors are over a dark (non-reflective) area or a white (reflective) surface. This means the sensors can be used to determine when the S3 is over a dark line on a white surface. With this capability we can write a program that can give the robot the ability to follow a line.

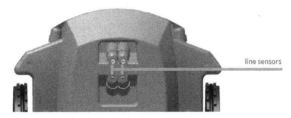

line sensors

Figure 7.1: The S3 has two line sensors on the bottom of the robot.

Developing with the Simulator
As in some of the previous chapters, we will use the simulator to help develop an *algorithm* (a plan) that can make the S3 follow a line. When we know the plan works with the simulation, we will modify the program so it controls the S3.

RobotBASIC programs can obtain a number representing the line-sensor data using the function **rSense()**. Remember, functions have value, they can be used in mathematical expressions just like a number or a variable. For example, we could store the sensor data in the variable **d** with the following statement.

```
d = rSense()
```

S3 has two line sensors, and later in this chapter we will utilize both sensors to create a much better line-following algorithm. Since we are still learning about sensor controlled behaviors though, it is important at this point to keep things simple. For that reason, for this project, we will view the two line sensors as if they are one large one. If the value of **rSense()** is zero, then neither of the line sensors are over a line. If the value is not zero, then at least one of the sensors *sees* the line.

Imagine you have a line on a piece of poster board and that you have a circular piece of paper with a small hole in it and that it is positioned so that you can see the line through the hole as in Figure 7.2. Think of the circular piece of paper as the S3 and that the hole in the paper represents the line sensor. Imagine that you are the robot and that the only thing you can see is whatever is visible through the hole – *you know you can see the line, or that you can't, nothing else* (you cannot tell, for example, if the line is on the left or right side of the hole). How would you follow the line with only this information?

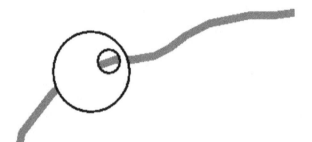

Figure 7.2: Imagine you are the robot.

Most people without programming experience offer an idea such as *move the paper in a circular motion and see which way the line is going, and then move in that direction*. That might work for a human, but remember, you are the robot. Moving in a circular motion would not be easy, and even if you could move like that it would be a very awkward way to follow the line.

As a robot, you can either turn to the right or left or you can move forward. With that in mind, think about this approach. If you can see the line through the hole, turn slightly to the right and move forward a little. For a fairly straight line, this will tend to put you (as the robot) to the right of the line. If you cannot see the line (meaning you have moved too far to the right) then you should turn left slightly and more forward again. Imagine if you repeated these two actions over and over. Can you see how these actions would move you in a path that would follow the line?

Think about this algorithm carefully. You, as the robot, are constantly moving forward, and when you see the line you turn right, taking you away from the line. When you have moved too far and don't see the line, you turn to the left, trying to find it again.

The program in Figure 7.3 implements these ideas for the simulator. This program is organized similarly from those you have seen so far. There is the main program and three other modules. The three subroutines in this program are named **InitRobot**, **DrawLine**, and **FollowLine**. As you would expect, these three subroutines initialize the robot, draw a line on the screen, and make the robot follow the line.

```
main:
  gosub DrawLine
  gosub InitRobot
  gosub FollowLine
end
InitRobot:
  rLocate 50,550
  rInvisible GREEN
  rSpeed 5
return

DrawLine:
  LineWidth 10
  SetColor GREEN
  Line 50,550,50,500
  LineTo 60,450
  LineTo 100,400
  LineTo 150,370
  LineTo 180,360
  LineTo 200,360
  LineTo 230,355
  LineTo 250,345
  LineTo 270,330
  LineTo 300,315
  LineTo 350,305
  LineTo 380,305
  LineTo 420,300
  LineTo 450,290
  LineTo 490,260
  LineTo 520,220
  LineTo 530,200
  LineTo 535,170
  LineTo 550,150
  LineTo 565,140
  LineTo 580,140
  LineTo 595,150
  LineTo 610,155
  LineTo 625,155
  LineTo 650,150
  LineTo 670,180
  LineTo 670,250
```

```
  LineTo 555,390
  LineTo 550,460
  LineTo 510,480
  LineTo 400,400
  LineTo 600,460
  LineTo 530,480
  LineTo 445,400
  LineWidth 1
return

FollowLine:
  while true
    if rSense(GREEN)=0
      rTurn -1
    else
      rTurn 1
    endif
    rForward 1
  wend
return
```

Figure 7.3: This program makes the simulated robot follow a line.

Look at the **main** program. From this small block of code, it is easy to see that this program does three things. It draws a line, initializes the robot, and then makes that robot follow the line. Now we can look at each subroutine individually to see how each task is accomplished. We will look first at the **DrawLine** module.

DrawLine starts by setting up a line width of 10 (so lines will be drawn 10 pixels wide) and a color of **GREEN** (so anything drawn, including lines, will be in green). The next line in the module draws a line from x,y position 50,550 to 50,500 (a vertical line whose length is 50 pixels). The next statement draws a line from the last point plotted (50,500) to 60,450. The rest of the module is a series of **LineTo** statements that completes the drawing of the line shown in Figure 7.4.

It is easy to see why the **DrawLine** module has so many statements. The line being drawn is fairly long and made up of many small segments. Notice that the beginning of the line (starting at the bottom left of the screen) is made up of slow gentle turns. When the upper right corner of the screen has been reached the line starts to have sharper turns, and they get even sharper as the line moves down the right side of the screen.

Since the robot is going to follow this line starting from the left, it will have a fairly easy line to follow in the beginning, but it will eventually have to contend with sharper turns, which are harder to follow.

The **InitRobot** module is much simpler. It locates the robot at position 50,150, which, if you remember, is the starting point for the line. Next, **GREEN** is specified as an invisible color so the simulated robot will not see the green line as an obstacle (allowing the robot to move over it like a line on the floor). Finally, the **rSpeed** command sets a delay of 5ms for each movement of the robot, which slows down the robot a little to make its movement easier to follow.

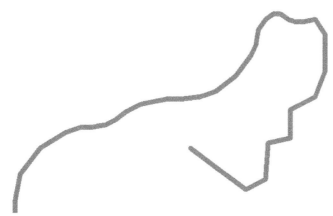

Figure 7.4: This is the line to be followed.

Following the Line

Now we are ready to examine the **FollowLine** module to see how the algorithm discussed earlier is actually implemented. Remember, that the algorithm was really simple. The robot, while moving forward, simply turns to the right if it sees the line and left if it doesn't.

Recall, that the S3 has two line sensors (RobotBASIC's standard simulated robot actually has three). The value of the line-sensor data, obtained with **rSense()**, can actually tell us the state of each of the sensors. Later in this chapter we will utilize this individualized information to develop a more robust line-following algorithm. For now though, we want to keep things simple, so we will assume our robots (both real and simulated) have only one line sensor. That means that a value of zero for **rSense()** means that no line is seen and any other value implies a line is seen.

Combining this numeric information with the algorithm discussed earlier now reduces to a simple statement: The robot (while moving forward) should turn to the left when **rSense()** is zero and to the right when it is not. This algorithm is not just easy to understand, but easy to implement. Look at the **FollowLine** subroutine in Figure 7.5.

Actually, **rSense()** on the simulator is designed to be able to follow lines of different colors, so since we are using a green line, we must use **rSense(GREEN)**.

Inside the subroutine itself, you first see a **while** loop that keeps the robot following the line *forever*. Inside the **while**-loop is an **IF-ELSE-ENDIF** control structure. If the value of **rSense(GREEN)** is zero (no line is seen) the **IF** will be **TRUE**, and an **rTurn -1** will turn the robot left. When a line is seen, the expression will be **FALSE**, and the **ELSE** block will execute an **rTurn 1** to turn the robot to the right.

Remember, the **rTurn** statement (for 1 and -1) on the simulator does not move the robot forward (it only rotates the robot left and right). For that reason, there is an **rForward 1** statement following the **IF** construct. This will advance the robot slightly after each turn. Run the program and you should see the robot follow the line as depicted by the path shown in Figure 7.5.

Notice the robot is staying on the right side of the line in Figure 7.5. Can you explain why? Can you make it follow on the left side? Notice also that the robot does a good job on gentle curves, but when the line makes a sharp turn, the robot loses the line. The robot actually does a pretty good job for only using one line sensor. Don't worry though, we will soon improve this program's performance.

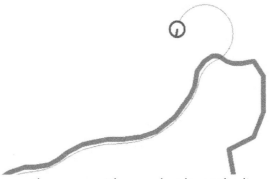

Figure 7.5: The robot handles gentle curves with ease, but loses the line when it turns sharply.

S3 Line Following

The next step is to modify the program in Figure 7.3 so that it will make the S3 follow a line. Of course, you will need a real line to follow since we will be using a real robot. Probably the easiest thing to do is to tape a couple of white poster or foam (preferred) boards together and make a line using black electrical tape (preferred) or magic marker as shown in Figure 7.6. Ideally the line should be about an inch wide. When using tape, be careful not to stretch it too much as it can cause poster board to curl (which is why foam board is preferred). Note: The S3 in Figure 7.6 has extra circuitry that will be discussed in a later chapter, but it is not required here.

Figure 7.6: Foam board and electrical tape makes creating a line easy.

Set **PortNum** equal to your Bluetooth port and modify the **InitRobot** module with an **rCommPort PortNum** command just as we have done in previous chapters. Since the **rTurn 1** and **rTurn -1** statements will make gentle turns (using the default turn style) while moving the S3 forward (as described in Chapter 4), we also need to remove the **rForward 1** statement from the **FollowLine** subroutine. If you run the program after this change, the S3 will respond just like the simulated robot – that is, if you place it on a line, it will follow the line as long as the curves are relatively gentle, just like the simulation. You don't need the **GREEN** specification in the **rSense()** function, but the S3 will simply ignore it if you don't remove it.

Make these modifications and verify the S3 can also follow lines. If your robot seems to be having problems it could be because your line is reflecting light back just like the white surface (only less, but enough that it might be confusing the sensors). This can easily happen with the ink in some brands of markers or if your black tape is too shiny. If this is a problem, a fix is provided at the end of this chapter.

Improving the Program

Our first attempt at following a line does a reasonably good job, but we can do better. Remember, this algorithm treated the line sensors on the simulator or the S3 as if they were only one big sensor. Let's see what we can do when we consider the sensors individually. Look at Figure 7.7.

The S3 will provide a sensor readings as shown in Figure 7.8. The simulated robot has three line sensors, so we need a way to use only two of them to mimic the S3. We can do that by modifying the **rSense()** function like this: **rSense()&5**. This makes the simulated robot ignore its middle sensor and only report the data from the two outside sensors. This makes the line data from the simulator mirror that from the S3 (figure 7.8).

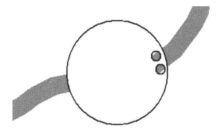

Figure 7.7: We can improve the line following behavior if we use both sensors.

New Algorithm

Think about how this expanded information can be used to follow a line. Look at Figure 7.7 and come up with your own ideas before reading further.

Sensor Value	Situation
0	no sensors see line
1	right sensor only, sees line
4	left sensor only, sees line
5	both sensors see line

Figure 7.8: These sensor values represent the situations shown.

It would seem we really have only three situations to deal with. If the sensor value is 5, the robot is well centered on the line and it can just move forward. If the value is 1 or 4, only one sensor is seeing the line, and the robot should turn to the left or right to move back to the center. Figure 7.9 shows how we can implement this idea.

When you run the program it produces the output shown in Figure 7.10. Unfortunately, the robot still loses the line, but compare this Figure to Figure 7.5 and you will see the new program keeps the robot in the center of the line instead of on the right side as in Figure 7.5.

The problem is that when the line curves quickly, even a small movement forward can get both sensors off the line. In the original program this always caused the robot to turn left. In this program the robot continues in a straight line. Examine both programs to figure out why.

The answer for the 2-sensor program is that the **IF** decision blocks do not check for the zero condition, which means the robot moves forward when the other **IF** blocks are false. The question is, what do we want the robot to do when it loses the line? What do you think?

```
FollowLine:
  while true
    a = rSense(GREEN)&5
    if a=4
      rTurn -1
    elseif a=1
      rTurn 1
    elseif a=5
      rForward 1
    endif
    rForward 1
  wend
return
```

Figure 7.9: This improved algorithm keeps the robot centered on the line.

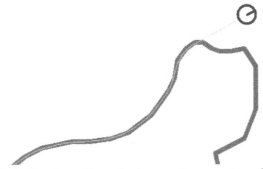

Figure 7.10: Notice how the robot now stays centered on the line.

Improving the Algorithm

Figure 7.11 shows an improved version of the 2-sensor **FollowLine**. The changes are outlined in **BOLD**. The new algorithm is exactly like the old algorithm except that it handles the situation where neither of the line sensors see the line. When that happens, we would like the robot to continue making the last turn it made before losing the line. And it should continue that turn as long as both sensors do not see the line, an action that brings the robot back to the center of the line.

The question becomes, *how do we know what the last turn was*? Look again at the figure. Every time a turn is made, the variable **Last** is made equal to the turn parameter. That way, all the new code has to do is **rTurn Last**.

If you make these changes to the program, the robot will perform as shown in Figure 7.12.

```
FollowLine:
  Last = 0
  while true
    a = rSense(GREEN)&5
    if a=4
      rTurn -1
      Last=-1
    elseif a=1
      rTurn 1
      Last=1
    elseif a=5
      rForward 1
    elseif a=0
      rTurn Last
    endif
    rForward 1 // remove for S3 operation
  wend
return
```

Figure 7.11: This version solves the line following problems.

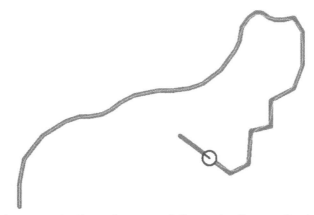

Figure 7.12: The robot now follows the line perfectly.

Analyzing the Program

You might be thinking we should have just applied the last-turn technique to the original program. If you study the original program though, you will see that we can't do that. The whole idea of the original line-follow was that the program turns to the right until it loses the line and then back to the left until it finds it again. When the line is lost, the robot MUST turn left.

In the new program though, the robot tries to stay in the middle of the line and this means it can lose the line on either side. By keeping track of which turn the robot was making when it lost the line, we know which way to turn to get back to the line.

Modify for the S3

Now that we have a great algorithm, modify the program appropriately and try it on your S3. At this point, you should be able to make these modifications on your own. If you have trouble, study the previous chapters to see how programs were modified to work with the S3.

Calibrating the Line Sensors

It was mentioned earlier that your robot might have problems detecting a line that is not dark enough or if it is too reflective. If you are using glossy black tape, for example, for your line, you might try rubbing it with steel wool or fine sandpaper to remove the gloss. If this does not work, there is an easy solution. The RROSS has a special **rCommand** that will cause the S3 to rotate 360° and take readings from the line sensors. The S3 will then automatically adjust the sensitivity of the sensors so that they work properly with the line you are using. Replace the original main program with the one in Figure 7.13 and add the new routine **CreateButtons** to your program. Run the new program, and you will get the output shown in Figure 7.14.

```
main:
  gosub CreateButtons
  gosub DrawLine
  gosub InitRobot
  SetTimeOut 10000 // lengthens communication timeout
  while TRUE
    GetButton ButtonName
    if ButtonName = "Calibrate" then rCommand(14,0)
    if ButtonName = "Follow Line"
      RemoveButton "Calibrate"
      RemoveButton "Follow Line"
      gosub FollowLine
    endif
  wend
end
```

```
CreateButtons:
  AddButton "Calibrate", 250,10
  AddButton "Follow Line", 350,10
return
```
Figure 7.13: This version of main creates two buttons as shown in Figure 7.14.

Note: A new command (**SetTimeOut 10000**) was used in Figure 7.13. Normally RobotBASIC gives an error if it does not received an expected communication in 5 seconds (5000ms). This command lengthens this time period to 10 seconds to ensure the robot has time to finish its calibration before it communicates with RobotBASIC. Do not confuse this command with setting the timeout period for the RROS which will be discussed later in the text.

Buttons
Buttons are created at a specific position on the screen with the **AddButton** command. The command **GetButton** will place the name of the last button pressed into the variable specified (**ButtonName** in this case). Your program can then check to see if **ButtonName** is the same as one of the buttons. Buttons can be removed with **RemoveButton**. Refer to the RobotBASIC HELP file for more information on button related commands.

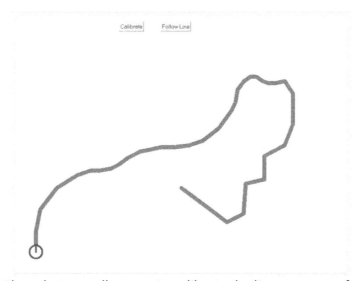

Figure 7.14: These buttons allow you to calibrate the line sensors or follow the line.

Notice at the top of the screen there are two buttons. The **Calibrate** button will not do anything on the simulation, but if works if you are controlling the S3. After running the program, just set the S3 so it is over a line. Press **Calibrate** and the robot will rotate one full revolution and adjust the sensor sensitivity as mentioned earlier. Calibration is performed using a special **rCommand** as shown in Figure 7.13. You can calibrate more than once if you wish. When ready, move the robot to the beginning of the line and click **Follow Line** and the buttons will disappear and the line-following behavior will begin. Note: The **Follow Line** button will work with either the S3 or the simulator.

This simple example with buttons demonstrates just one of many reasons why RobotBASIC is such a powerful tool for controlling your robot. The HELP file discusses hundreds of other great commands and functions that can make your programs easier to use and more fun to write. Remember, a printed book version of the HELP file is available on Amazon.com for those preferring the convenience of a hard copy.

Again, it is up to you to modify this final version of the line-following program so that it will work with the S3. When you have the programming working, you can improve its performance with a little tweaking.

Tweaking for Performance

You already know how to use an **rCommand** to alter the way the S3 makes turns for parameters of 1 and -1. The default for the S3 turn-style is to reduce the slow wheel to 50% of the faster wheel. The line-following program discussed here will work with this 50% turn, because when it loses the line, it makes a slow turn back until it finds the line again. If you are using a line with significant curves though, the robot can take a while to get back to the line. For that reason, the robot will perform better if you make the robot turn faster when trying to find the line. You can do this by reducing the speed of the slow wheel, perhaps **rCommand(1,20)** to run the slow wheel at only 20% of the faster wheel.

In some cases, the robot might perform better if you slowed it down. The default value for the S3's speed is 50% of maximum and this is ideal because it makes the robot perform very much like the simulation for some maneuvers. Previous chapters have discussed an **rCommand** that changes the turn style of the S3. There is also an **rCommand** that allows you to choose robot's speed. For example, **rCommand(2,40)** sets the speed to 40% of maximum. Try different speeds and turn styles to see if you can improve on your S3's line-following ability.

Making rCommand Easier to Use

As you have seen, there are two parameters used with **rCommand**s. The first parameter given to the **rCommand** is a command code. The code 1 is used to change the turn style and a code of 2 is used to change the speed. Remember also, a code of 14 was used earlier in this chapter for calibrating the line sensors and there was even a code for playing sounds. That means we now have four **rCommand**s that can provide special features – and there are more.

The way we have been using the **rCommand** makes it difficult to read unless you memorize all the command codes. Look at the new **InitS3** routine shown in Figure 7.15. The first two lines in the module initialize the S3 as we have done the past. The third line clears the screen since we don't really need to see the simulated robot when controlling the S3. The rest of this routine initializes the value of numerous variables.

These variables can be used to make the **rCommand** more friendly. For example, instead of using **rCommand(2,70)** to set the S3's speed to 70% of maximum, we can use this:

```
rCommand(SetSpeed, 70)
```

This works because the variable **SetSpeed** is set equal to 2 in the **InitS3** subroutine (see Figure 7.15). Since **SetSpeed** is a variable, it must be typed exactly like it appears in the subroutine, including capitalization. When you see this command in a program, you know immediately what the **rCommand** is doing. When you are programming, and want to change the speed, you don't have to look up the code (it is much easier to remember that **SetSpeed** sets the speed than it is that 2 sets the speed, especially if there are a lot of codes).

There are many new codes listed in Figure 7.15. They will be introduced when needed throughout this text. Appendix A also provides a quick summary of purpose of each **rCommand**. Of course, it does not save you a lot of time and aggravation if you need to type in the InitS3 module every time you start a new program.

```
InitS3:
  rCommPort PortNum
  rLocate 100,100
                            // default value (0-255) or info
  SetTurnStyle        = 1   // 50 (slow wheel at this %
  SetSpeed            = 2   // 50 (% of maximum speed)
  DriveRightCurve     = 5   // provide radius (.5 inch units)
  SetHalfDriveDegrees = 8   // 360 (how far to drive)
  PixelMultiplier     = 9   // 1 (2, doubles the range readings)
  DriveLeftCurve      = 10  // provide radius (.5 inch units)
  PlaySound           = 11  // provide freq (/ by multiplier)
  CalibLineSensors    = 14  // rotates robot (over line)
  SetFreqMult         = 15  //    10
  SetDur              = 16  // 50 (500ms, units of 10ms)
  SetVSSmode          = 17  // provide range (cm units)
  SetTMout            = 18  // 20 (units of 10ms gives 200ms)
  ReadPings           = 19  // 1st 3 bytes, in returned string
  ReadAnalog          = 20  // 2 bytes each, MSB first
  ReadLight           = 21  // 1st 4 bytes contain light data
  ExpandFeel          = 22  // 0,expand Feel with digital sensors
  SetBumpDist         = 23  // default is half the FEEL distance
  Bumpers             = 128 // use with SetVSSmode to add bumpers
  Dual                = 64  // use with SetVSSmode to also use IR
return
```
Figure 7.15: This subroutine make working with the S3 even easier.

Using the InitS3 Module
There are actually three easy ways to incorporate the InitS3 module into your programs. First, you can either type it in once (and save it alone as InitS3.bas) or you can download a copy from RobotBASIC.org (see the **Parallax Scribbler S3** tab). Once you have this program stored on your computer, you can just OPEN it when you want to start a new program and then SAVE it using a

name appropriate for your new program. This way you start off with this module as a part of your program – just insert your new program code at the beginning of the file.

If you have already started a program and want to add an **InitS3** module to your code, you can click on the **File** menu and choose **Merge To End**, and select the file InitS3.bas from your disk. It will added to your program at the end of the current code.

The third way of incorporating **InitS3** in your program is to add the following line to the very beginning of your code.

```
#include "InitS3.bas"
```

This new command will effectively merge the file at the end of your code, but it will not be visible to you. It will be there though, and you can use it the same as if you had typed it in. The advantage of using **#include** files is that your code is smaller and easier to scroll through etc. You can use this technique to create entire libraries of subroutines that you can easily utilize in your programs. If you are new to programming though, I would suggest you use one of the first two methods described above. Being able to see the module you are calling can be comforting for beginners. It is also import to know that include files should be fully debugged, because you cannot step though included code and if an error ever occurs in the code, you will be told about the error, but you won't be able to see it (because include files are not visible to you).

Developing Algorithms

This chapter provides many insights into how algorithms are developed. The original line-following algorithm used only one sensor and it was easy to understand and implement. Using two sensors allowed the algorithm to be improved but still not enough to handle sharp turns.

When the problem was analyzed, it became evident that the robot's performance could be enhanced if the robot, when it loses the line, could continue turning in the same direction it was turning *before* it lost the line. The reader was then encouraged to improve the program even more by experimenting with the robot's speed and turn style parameters.

The real point is that there are *many* ways to make your robot solve most problems. Always *think* about a problem and its solution before you try to write your program. Even when you get a program working, it can be valuable to analyze what is happening and experiment with new ideas and options to make the algorithm even better.

This kind of activity is what programming is all about. For many people, *analyzing* and *improving* are exciting activities that make programming enjoyable and stimulating. If you feel this way, you might consider a career in programming or engineering.

Chapter 8
Ranging Sensors: Measuring Distance

So far we have written programs that utilized the S3's IR proximity sensors to detect objects in front of the robot, the light sensors to allow the robot to find and track a bright light, and finally the reflective line sensors on the bottom of the robot to allow it to follow a line. We can really improve on the S3's sensory capabilities if we enhance the S3 with new and more capable sensors.

Adding a Ranging Sensor

Let's start by adding an ultrasonic ranging sensor. Figure 8.1 shows a Parallax Ping sensor. It can be purchased from www.Parallax.com. The sensor works by sending out high-frequency sound waves (above the human hearing range) and measuring the time it takes for the sound to bounce off objects and return to the sensor.

Figure 8.1: This ultrasonic sensor can measure distances to objects.

Mount and wire your Ping sensor as described in Chapter 2. If you are only planning on adding one Ping sensor to your S3 to keep costs low, your robot should look something like Figure 8.2. If you are planning on mounting three Pings to maximize your S3's capabilities, you should just skip mounting a single Ping and mount the three sensors as described in Chapter 2 and shown in Figure 8.3. All the single-Ping projects in this book will work fine with either setup. There will, however, be some projects that require multiple Pings. When possible, reasonable work-arounds will be provided for those readers that do not have three Pings.

Figure 8.2: A single Ping sensor can be mounted on your robot as shown.

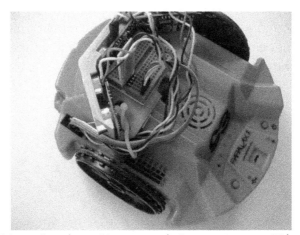

Figure 8.3: Mounting three Pings greatly improves your S3's capabilities.

Obtaining and Using the Ranging Data

The program in Figure 8.5 moves the robot forward until it is 10 centimeters from an obstacle (the default units returned by **rRange()** from the S3 are centimeters). After initialization, a **while**-loop continually moves the robot forward in tiny increments as long as the expression in the **while**-statement is true. This means the robot will continue to move forward as long as the Ping sensor returns a distance greater than 10 (10 pixels for the simulation, 10 cm for the S3).

Real vs Simulation

The program in Figure 8.5 will work with both the real robot and the simulator. It assumes you have the **InitS3** module from Chapter 7, Figure 1.15, included in your program. Let's start by setting **PortNum** equal to zero and watch the simulated robot. It will move forward until it is 10 pixels from the upper wall on the computer screen, as shown in Figure 8.6. If you set **PortNum** equal to the Bluetooth port for your robot, the S3 will move forward until it is 10 cm from some object blocking its path.

```
PortNum = 0 // set to your Bluetooth Port for the S3
           // set to zero to control simulation
main:
  if PortNum > 0
    gosub InitS3
  else
    rLocate 400,300
  wend
  while rRange()>10
    rForward 1
  wend
end

// Add your InitS3 routine here
```
Figure 8.5: This program will moved the robot forward until it reaches a wall.

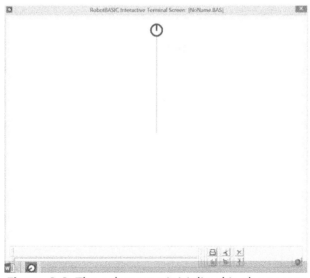

Figure 8.6: The robot was initialized in the center of the screen and moves until it reaches a wall.

If you are using the real robot place objects in front of it to verify it always stops when it sees them. Note: The sound waves must bounce back to be seen, so it is possible that a very soft stuffed animal might absorb the sound, or an angled wall might reflect it away from the robot. If you are using the simulator, you can draw objects to block the robot's movements as you've seen in previous chapters.

As you will see, the robot (both real and simulated) will stop when it encounters an object. The difference between the ranging sensor and the IR perimeter proximity sensors used in earlier chapters, is that now we can stop, not just when an object is detected, but at a desired distance from the object. Try creating objects on the screen or locating the robot in a lower position to test the simulation. Make objects on the screen GREEN and verify the robot does not see them.

Change the **main** program in Figure 8.5 so that it looks like Figure 8.7. This new version of the program continually prints the distance measured by the Ping sensor. Run the program and move your hand closer to the robot and watch the distance change on the screen. Try moving your hand left and right. You will see that the sound beam used for the ultrasonic Ping sensors is considerably wider than the standard IR beam on the S3.

Note: The two extra spaces printed in the **xyString** statement prevent errors in the display. If you did not do this, the ending digits in a long number can still be displayed with smaller numbers. For example, if the distance displayed was 123 and suddenly it became 8, the new number displayed would be 823, because the 2 and the 3 would still be on the screen from the last reading.

```
main:
  gosub InitS3
  while TRUE
    xyString 10,10,rRange()," "
  wend
end
```

Figure 8.7: This version of the program continually displays the measured distance

In order to better demonstrate how the Ping sensor can be used, let's create a program that can scan the area around the robot (either the simulation or the S3). Our new program is going to use array variables though, so let's discuss them first.

Array Variables

Having named variables is nice for holding small amounts of data. What if we needed 100 or even a 1000 variables to store information? It is hard to imagine how you could think of so many names and even harder to write programs to efficiently manipulate so much information. This is why programmers need *arrays*.

You can reserve space for array variables with the DIM statement (stands for dimension, and can be used to create arrays of one or many dimensions). Look at the demonstration program in Figure 8.8. The first line of this program reserves space for 20 *elements* under the name **R**. The first item is **R[0]**, then **R[1], R[2],** etc. all the way up to **R[19]**. Note that the first element is 0, not 1. One of the great things about arrays is that we can also reference a specific element in an array with a variable. For example, **A[x]** refers to an element based on the value of **x**. If **x** is 3, for example, the expression is referring to **A[3]**. This ability to reference an array element with a variable (or even a mathematical expression) makes it possible to write small programs that do a lot of manipulation.

Look at the first **FOR**-loop in Figure 8.8. It makes the variable **i** vary from 0 to 19 (all the elements of the array **R[ ]**. Inside the loop, each element of the array is assigned a random number between 0 and 100. The second loop prints the 20 numbers as shown in Figure 8.9.

```
Dim R[20]
for i=0 to 19
  R[i] = random(100)
next

for i=0 to 19
  print R[i]
next
```

Figure 8.8: Arrays provide an easy way to manipulate large amounts of data.

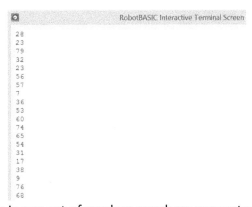

Figure 8.9: This is one set of random numbers generated by Figure 8.8.

If you change the last **FOR**-loop in Figure 8.8 as shown in Figure 8.10, the program will print the numbers in two columns (see Figure 8.11). Notice how mathematical formulas are used to control where the numbers are printed and actually which numbers are printed. The first formula, for example, starts the first column 200 pixels over and 100 pixels down, with a spacing of 20 pixels between lines. The semicolon (instead of a comma between the two array elements) *tabs* over for the second column and the expression **i+10** prints the array elements 10 through 19 as the loop variable **i** transitions from 0 to 9.

```
for i=0 to 9
  xyString 200,100+20*i,R[i];R[i+10]
next
```

Figure 8.10: This modification prints the random numbers in two columns.

RobotBASIC Interactive Terminal Screen	
28	60
23	74
79	65
32	54
23	31
56	17
57	38
7	9
36	76
53	68

Figure 8.11: It is easy to create a two-column output.

Let's look at one final example with Arrays before we get back to scanning with the Ping sensor. Figure 8.12 shows a code fragment that you can add to the very end of the previous example. It uses a loop to add every element in the array together in the variable **tot** and then divides the total by 20. Note that 20.0 was used to force a floating point divide. If you use only 20, the average will be rounded off to an integer.

Try modifying the program so that it creates 60 random numbers, prints the numbers in two columns and the average at the bottom of the columns. Once you get that to work, modify it so that the numbers are displayed in 3 columns of 20 each.

```
tot = 0
for i=0 to 19
  tot = tot+R[i]
next
print
print
print "Total = ",tot
print "Average = ",tot/20.0
```

Figure 8.12: This code Fragment find the average of the numbers in the array.

The important point is that loops and arrays make it possible to manipulate huge amounts of data with tiny amounts of code. As you learn more about programming, this power will become more and more apparent. Now that you have been introduced to arrays, let's get back to scanning with a Ping sensor.

Scanning the Area Around the Robot

The program in Figure 8.13 is our starting point. Notice the main program is very short because it simply calls other modules to handle the tasks that needed to be done. The program has been designed to work with either the **S3** or the simulated robot (just use a **PortNum** of zero). Let's start by using only the simulation.

```
#include "InitS3.bas" // or merge into your program
main:
  PortNum = 0
  Dim Dist[12]
  if PortNum=0 then gosub DrawEnvironment
  gosub InitRobot
  gosub Scan
  gosub ShowScan
end

DrawEnvironment:
  circle 340,100,390,150,BLACK,BLACK
  circle 300,450,550,525,BLACK,BLACK
  rectangle 125,400,225,550,BLACK,BLACK
  rectangle 550,200,700,330,BLACK,BLACK
return

Scan:
  angle = 0
  for i = 0 to 11
    Dist[i]= rRange()
    rTurn -30
  next
return

ShowScan:
  angle = 0
  for i=0 to 11
    a=DtoR(angle)// convert degrees to radians for trig functions
    line 400,300,400+(Dist[i]*cos(a)),300-(Dist[i]*sin(a))
    angle = angle+30
  next
return

InitRobot:
  if PortNum>0
    gosub InitS3
  else
    rLocate 400,300,90 // faces the robot 90 degrees to the right
    rInvisible GREEN
    rPen Down
  endif
return
```

Figure 8.13: This program directs the robot to scan the area around it.

The Robot's Environment

If you run the program, you will see the screen shown in Figure 8.14. Notice the four shapes that have been placed throughout the screen. Examine the code in the **DrawEnvironment** module of Figure 8.13 to see how each of the shapes are created. Notice also that the robot is located in the center of the screen and turned to the right. This orientation of the robot makes the needed math more straightforward because 0 degrees (for trigonometry functions) is to the right as in a graph.

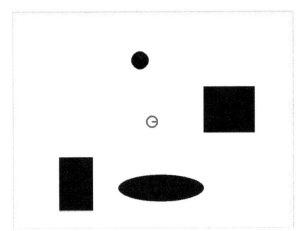

Figure 8.14: This is the environment for the simulated robot.

Ultrasonic vs Infrared

As discussed in previous chapters, the Ping sensor works by sending out sound waves and watching for them to bounce off objects and return. Ping is not the only type of ranging sensor available. Some rangers use a beam of infrared light to detect objects and measure how far away they are.

The reason this is important is that while both types of ranging sensor measure distance, the beam on the IR sensor is very narrow and can only detect objects directly in front of the sensor. The sound waves on ultrasonic sensors though, spread out in a cone shape. Both sensors can only detect objects hit by their beam, but the wider cone-shaped ultrasonic beam allows it to detect objects that are off to the side slightly as shown in Figure 8.15. In many situations, this makes ultrasonic rangers more useful. Note: IR sensors can sometimes have trouble seeing dark or otherwise non-reflective objects, and ultrasonic sensors can have trouble with soft objects that might absorb sound.

The simulated robot handles its ranging operation more like an IR sensor (it only checks for objects in a straight line). This means that an IR scan (like that of the simulator) can miss objects. Look at the **Scan** module in Figure 8.13.

The **Scan** module simply rotates the robot through 12 positions of 30° each. At each position, the measurement from **rRange()** is stored in the next element of the array **Dist[ ]**. We could print these out, but the information can be easier to visualize if we display it graphically.

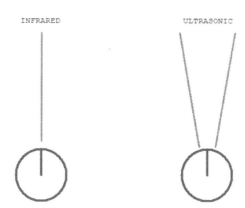

Figure 8.15: Ultrasonic rangers have a wider beam than IR.

The **ShowScan** module uses trigonometry to draw lines equal to the scan distances stored in the array. If you are not familiar with the math, simply accept that that the module draws the lines as described. They are shown in Figure 8.16. Notice the lines are shorter where the objects are detected. Notice also that the round object at the top of the screen is in between two of the beams, so it is not seen.

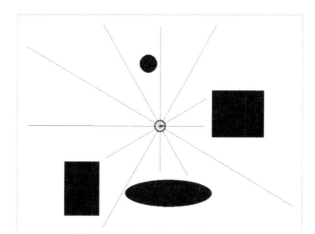

Figure 8.16: These lines represent the distances measured at each position.

Figure 8.17 shows three arcs that indicate the areas the scan readings imply are open for travel (because at least one scan distance is long). Since the round object mentioned earlier is not see, there is a huge area at the top and top-left of the screen that the robot thinks is open. Another error associated with this scan is the bottom-left. Since a scan penetrated between two objects, it is easy to assume the area is open, when in fact is not.

If we must use IR rangers, we could have the robot take more than 12 readings. This would not be necessary though, if we had the wider beam of the Ping sensors. In order to use the simulator for development with Pings, we need a way for the simulated robot to use a beam more like the S3. Luckily, this is also easy to do.

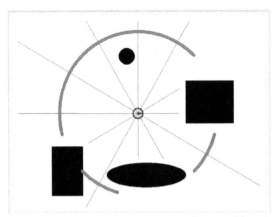

Figure 8.17: The arcs show open areas as deemed by the scan data.

Emulating an Ultrasonic Ranger

Look at Figure 8.17. It is a subroutine that can make the simulator act like it has an ultrasonic ranger. It starts by setting the variable **D** equal to the first **rRange()** reading taken. A **FOR**-loop then takes 40 range readings at various angles to form a wide beam and makes **D** equal to the smallest value obtained. This is equivalent to what a Ping would do (the signal reflected from the closest object will trigger the sensor first and terminate the reading).

```
UltraSonicDistance:
  D = rRange() // sets an initial value for D
  for angle = -20 to 20
    d = rRange(angle)
    if d<D then D = d
  next
return
```

Figure 8.17: This subroutine emulates an ultrasonic ranger.

We can use this new routine in the original program by replacing the line **Dist[i] = rRange()** in the **Scan** module with the following lines:

```
gosub UltraSonicDistance
Dist[i] = D
```

These lines execute the subroutine which puts the range information in the variable **D**, which is why the value of **D** is then stored in the appropriate array element. If we run this new version of the program, the output will be as shown in Figure 8.18. The arcs have again been added to show where the scan data indicates the open spaces are.

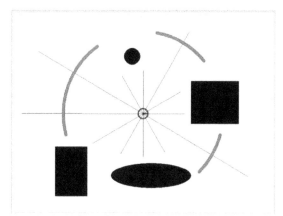

Figure 8.18: The ultrasonic scan more accurately
detects the open areas in the environment.

Notice, the wider beams now see the circular object at the top of the screen and the tiny opening between the two lower objects is interpreted correctly as blocked. Compare this scan with the faulty one in Figure 8.16.

Reusable Modules

In Chapter 6 it was mentioned that one advantage of modular code is that you can often copy a subroutine from one program and use it in a different program (either as is or with minor modifications). While this is a great idea, in practice there can be problems with this approach.

One such problem is variables. So far in our programs, all our variables are *global*, that is to say that any variable (for example, the variable **x**) is the same variable everywhere in the program. In many cases, this is a very good thing, but not always. Let's look at the **UltraSonicDistance** routine in Figure 8.17. The variable **D** needs to be global because it is used to convey the distance obtained to other areas of the program. The other variables (**d** and **angle**) are only needed *inside* this routine. The problem is: If you paste this subroutine in another program, it might not work. Why? If the new program also uses variables named **D**, **d** and **angle**, then when this subroutine changes these values, it would *also* change the values of these variables *everywhere* in the program and that could cause errors. To ensure this routine will work in a new program, you would have to search the entire program to check if there are any variable conflicts – and if you find some, change the names of the duplicate variables.

Having to modify the names of variables in this way could make reusing a previously written subroutine more of a chore than something helpful. As we will soon see, RobotBASIC provides an easy way to solve this problem. Before we look at the solution though, let's look at one more problem with reusable routines.

As mentioned, when you copy and paste a routine from one program to another, you might have to edit it in some way because it does not exactly do what you want it to do. For example, you might want the **UltraSonicDistance** module to check for more or less than the 40° scan we used or you might prefer that it placed the answer it obtains in a different variable. You might even want to scan a totally different range of angles. Of course, you could edit the routine, but it would be better if these options could be obtained without any editing whatsoever.

A Solution

Figure 8.19 shows a small program that demonstrates a special kind of *sub-routine* (to differentiate it from a *subroutine*) that solves all of the problems discussed above. Let's first see how to use it, then we will see how it works.

```
main:
  rLocate 400,500
  x=100   // coordinates and radius of ball
  y=100
  r=30
  while TRUE
    call UltraSonicRange(-20, 20,measurement)
    if measurement<100
      xyString 50,50,"I see an object    "
    else
      xyString 50,50,"No objects close by"
    endif
    gosub MoveBall
  wend
end

sub UltraSonicRange(a1, a2 ,&Dist)
  Dist=rRange()
  for angle = a1 to a2
    r = rRange(angle)
    if r<Dist then Dist = r
  next
return

MoveBall:
  LineWidth 5
  circle x-r,y-r,x+r,y+r,WHITE,WHITE
  ReadMouse x,y,b
  circle x-r,y-r,x+r,y+r,RED,BLUE
return
```

Figure 8.19: This sub-routine makes it easy to create reusable code.

In the **main** routine the simulated robot is initialized and the **x,y** coordinates and radius (**r**) of a ball are established. When the program is run, you will see a screen similar to that shown in Figure 8.20. When you move the mouse around the screen, a ball will follow the mouse cursor as it moves. We will see how this happens shortly. For now, it is suggested that you run the program to get a feel for what it does so that the following explanation might make more sense.

Figure 8.20: As you move the ball with the mouse, the program displays whether it sees the ball or not.

An endless **while**-loop does the work. It starts by **CALL**ing a special sub-routine named **UltraSonicRange** (instead of **GOSUB**ing to it). The rest of the line shows the numbers -20, 20, and the variable **measurement**. The numbers specify the desired angular range for the beam area we want to scan. The next item specifies the name of the variable where we want the sub-routine to place the answer (the shortest distance measured to objects within the beam).

Next, inside an endless loop, an **IF** statement displays if objects are seen or not depending on whether **measurement** is less than 100. Don't worry about the rest of the program for now. Just study the **main** code to see how easy this new routine is to *use*. The great thing about this routine is that you can make it scan a beam with designated start and stop angles, and place the distance measured into any variable you choose. Plus, there will never be any conflicts between variables used inside the routine and those elsewhere in the program. For example, there is a variable **r** in the main program (the radius of the ball) and a variable **r** in the sub-routine (holds the range measured). Even though these variables have the same name, they are different variables and changing one has no effect on the other. Variables used inside of sub-routines are *local* variables and are not related to any other variable in the program, even if it has the same name.

Run the program and move the ball around with your mouse and notice how wide the scanning beam seems to be, and how close objects have to be to be detected. Then edit the program and make the beam wider or narrower and change how close the ball must be to be seen. Move the ball again to see the difference.

Inside the SUB-routine

Now that you understand how to use this routine let's see how easy it is to create it. Look at the line that reads **sub UltraSonicRange(a1, a2, &Dist)**. The **sub** is a directive telling RobotBASIC this is a special type of routine. The first variable (**a1**) inside the parenthesis will assume the first value provided in the **CALL** statement by either a variable or a number (-20 in this example). The second variable (**a2**) will assume the next value passed (20 in this example).

The next item in parenthesis is different because it starts with an **&**. In this case, the **&** is saying whenever RobotBASIC see this variable (**Dist**) inside of this sub-routine, it should actually use the variable whose name is passed in the **CALL** statement. For this program this means that whatever value is assigned to **Dist** inside of the sub-routine will actually be assigned to the global variable **measurement** in the **main** program.

Inside of the sub-routine, we see similar code that was in the original subroutine for the simulator. The **FOR**-loop generates all the angles within the requested beam width by starting with **a1** and ending with **a2**. These angles are then used with **rRange()** to scan every position within the beam width. Only the shortest of these readings is remembered in **Dist**, which, as far as the main program knows, is actually the variable **measurement**. All this seems complicated, but everything is handled by RobotBASIC.

Any variables inside this sub-routine (like **a1, a2, angle, r**, and **Dist** for instance) are only valid inside the routine itself. You can have another variables with the same names elsewhere in the program and they are not affected by what you do to inside the routine. This means you can paste this routine into any program and use like we did in **main**, without having to worry if you have variable conflicts. The variables used inside of the sub-routine are often referred to as *local* variables (as opposed to the *global* variables in the rest of the program). And you should not have to edit this routine because you can control the width of the beam you want by just changing what you pass it.

Now for the Ball

I am hoping that most readers are a little curious about how the mouse moves the ball around on the screen. It is actually much easier than you probably imagine. Look at the **MoveBall** subroutine in Figure 8.19. It starts by drawing a circle of radius **r** at position **x,y**. But look carefully, it draws this circle totally in **WHITE**, which effectively erases the *last place* the ball was. The **ReadMouse** routine then makes **x** and **y** equal to the current position of the mouse and draws a blue ball (circle) with a red boarder at that new position. The next time the routine is run, it will erase this newly drawn ball and then draw it in a new position dictated by the mouse. If this seems confusing, comment out the line that erases the ball and run the program. You will see something like Figure 8.21 because a new ball is drawn wherever the mouse is, but the old one is never erased.

Figure 8.21: If you do not erase the ball, it leaves a trail as you move the mouse.

Sub-routines can be a fantastic tool in the hands of an experienced programmer. If you are new to programming and are confused by this discussion, then just continue to use the old-style subroutines. As the programs we write get larger, the value of sub-routines increases too.

Using the SUB-routine in the Original Program

Add the sub-routine from Figure 8.19 to the original program in the chapter, and replace the **Dist[i] = rRange()** in the **Scan** module with the following code:

```
call UltraSonicRange(-20,20,D)
Dist[i]=D
```

If you set **PortNum** to your Bluetooth port, the program will make the **S3** scan the area around it. Figure 8.22 shows the **S3** with various walls and obstacles surrounding it. (The walls are made from foam board and the obstacles are cut-down oat boxes as seen in previous chapters.) Figure 8.23 shows the scan output in the same orientation as Figure 8.20. Notice how the scan lines correspond nicely with the physical setup, showing three open areas.

Figure 8.22: The program used for the simulator can direct the **S3** to scan the area around it.

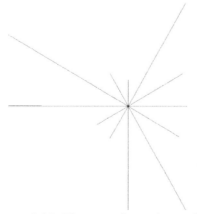

Figure 8.23: The scan lines drawn by the program correspond to the objects in Figure 8.20.

If you want to duplicate the scan in Figure 8.23 for your robot, just change **PortNum** to the one used for your Bluetooth. You may want to scale the length of the lines drawn by multiplying the numbers in the Array by a suitable constant, perhaps 3 or 4 (depends on the size of your real environment.

Libraries
If you use the sub-routine format to create routines to control your robot, you can place them all in a separate program and name it something like **LibraryRoutines.bas**. You can either copy and paste routines from that program (open it in a separate tab in RobotBASIC) into your target program, or just **#include** it so that all the routines will be accessible. Remember, if you have questions about subjects being covered, consult the RobotBASIC HELP file.

Multiple Ping Sensors
Everything in this chapter used only a single Ping sensor pointing forward. If you have three Ping sensors on your **S3** as described in Chapter 2, you can access the front one with **rRange()** or **rRange(0)**. Providing a negative parameter will access the left sensor and numbers greater than zero will access the right sensor.

Chapter 9
Following a Wall

If a robot has a ranging sensors, it is capable of more exciting behaviors. Ideally, your **S3** will have three rangers as described in Chapter 2 but even with only one, many of the activities in this chapter are still attainable. If you only have only one ranger though, you *must* mount it so that it points about 45-55 degrees to the left of the **S3** and wire it as the left sensor. If you do not have any rangers on your robot, you can still learn the principles outlined in this chapter using the simulator. The goal of this chapter is to program a robot to follow the contours of a wall and in future chapters that ability will be combined with other behaviors to demonstrate how rudimentary machine behaviors can be built in layers.

Using the Simulator for Development

As in previous chapters, RobotBASIC's simulator will be used to develop the algorithm that will govern the robot's behavior. Once we have developed the principles of wall-following with the simulation, we will transfer those ideas to the **S3**.

Let's start with the program in Figure 9.1. The main section of code performs four tasks by calling subroutines to draw walls to be followed, initialize the robot, find a wall, and follow that wall. Two of these subroutines are actually completed in the figure.

The **DrawWall** routine uses three circle commands to create a blob-like shape with an exterior edge (wall) that has a variety of interior and exterior curves. The **InitRobot** routine simply locates the simulated robot on the screen and drops a pen so we can see its movements.

The **FindWall** and **FollowWall** routines have been left blank at this time, but will be developed soon. If we run the program shown in Figure 9.1, it will draw the output shown in Figure 9.2. Examine it to see how **DrawWall** uses circles and ellipses to create the blob mentioned earlier. One of the great things about using a simulation is that it is easy to create a wide variety of environmental conditions for experimentation. Once our wall-following behavior is working, you can easily create a more complex wall for further testing. You will find though, that the variety associated with this shape is complex enough that it serves as a reasonable testing platform.

Notice from Figure 9.2 that the robot has been located a short distance from the wall itself. It is facing the wall though, so it will be easy for us to create the **FindWall** routine. Before you proceed further in this chapter, pause for a short time and think of how *you* would write the **FindWall** routine. Start with deciding *what* you want the robot to do and then think about *how* you can write code to make the robot perform the way you want.

```
main:
  gosub DrawWall
  gosub InitRobot
  gosub FindWall
  gosub FollowWall
end

DrawWall:
  Circle 250,200,500,300,RED,RED
  Circle 300,100,550,250,RED,RED
  Circle 350,250,450,350,RED,RED
return

InitRobot:
  rLocate 300,500
  rInvisible GREEN
  rPen DOWN
return

FindWall:
return

FollowWall:
return
```

Figure 9.1: This code outlines the basic template for our wall-following program.

Figure 9.2: This output is produced by the program in Figure 9.1.

Finding the Wall

So what should the robot do to find the wall? Since we can assume (for this example) that the robot is facing the wall, the behavior needed is to simply move forward until it gets close to the wall. Figure 9.3 shows how readings from the range sensor can be used to determine when to stop the robot.

A **while**-loop continually moves the robot forward in tiny 1-pixel movements as long as the distance to the wall is larger than 12 pixels. Try experimenting with different numbers to control when to stop, but change the program back to 12 when you are finished as a value of 12 seems to stop the simulated robot at a reasonable distance from the wall. Figure 9.4 shows how the robot actually moves to the wall using the code in Figure 9.3. Note that there is no angle in the **rRange()** statement, so it looks directly forward. This is the same as giving it the parameter **0**.

```
FindWall:
  While rRange()>12
    rForward 1
  wend
return
```
Figure 9.3: This version of **FindWall** moves the robot forward while it is too far from wall.

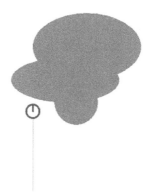

Figure 9.4: The code in Figure 8.3 moves the robot as shown here.

The Real Work

Now that we have a wall drawn, and the robot adjacent to it, we are ready to get down to business and make the robot follow the contours of the wall. Again, start by decided *what* you want the robot to do. A good way to do this is to place yourself in the robot's position. What would *you* do to follow a wall?

Imagine you are blindfolded or in a totally dark room. Assume you have moved forward, until you are close to a wall (just like our robot). How would *you* follow the wall? Think about this before reading further.

Developing the Algorithm

Hopefully you decided that following a wall is pretty easy in a dark room. If someone put you next to a wall in a dark room, you probably would reach out with one hand and use it to stay close to the wall as you walk forward. If you get too close to the wall (your arm is bent), you move away from the wall. If you get too far from the wall (your hand is no longer touching), you move closer. This very simple idea is exactly what we want the robot to do. Figure 9.5 shows a good first approach to solving this problem.

```
FollowWall:
  rTurn 90
  while TRUE
    if rRange(-90)>50
      rTurn -1
    else
      rTurn 1
    endif
    rForward 1
  wend
return
```

Figure 9.5: This version of FollowWall, follows the wall nicely, for a while.

The version of **FollowWall** in Figure 9.5 starts by turning the robot 90° to the right in order to generally align it with the wall. An endless **while**-loop checks the distance to the wall by using the simulated range sensor on the robot's left side. If the robot is further than 50 pixels away, the robot turns back toward the wall. Otherwise, the robot turns away from the wall. After a turn (either toward or away from the wall) the robot moves forward slightly. Note the similarity of this code to you feeling your way along a wall in a dark room as described earlier.

Unfortunately, if you assemble this program and run it, it produces the results shown in Figure 9.6. The robot does indeed begin to following the wall properly. But, as you can see, when the robot encounters an abrupt protrusion in the wall's contour, it collides causing an error. Part of the problem is that the wall being followed actually turns to the left when the robot needs to be turning right (see the Figure).

As a programmer, the next step is to understand exactly why the algorithm failed and propose one or more possible solutions. The solutions, of course have to be tested to see if they work or have the potential to work (which leads to more proposals and more testing).

Before reading on, examine the code and the output and come up with some ways you think might fix the problem.

Possible Solutions
One possible solution is to make the robot follow the wall in the same manner, but to stay further from it. If you increase the distance from 50 to 60 you will see an improvement, but the collision still occurs. If you get to 70 though, the robot is far enough out that it succeeds as shown in Figure 9.7.

Unfortunately, the fix is only good for this particular wall. If we make the circle obstructing the robot's path a bit wider, as shown in Figure 9.8, the robot fails just like before. Obviously we need a better solution. Can you think of one?

Figure 9.6: The robot follows the wall until it reaches a protrusion.

Figure 9.7: Move the robot further from the wall seems to work.

Figure 9.8: Changing the wall results in same error as before.

A Better Solution

What is really needed is for the robot to be looking ahead so it can start turning before it gets too close to the wall. That is *what* needs to be done. Now we just need to figure out *how* to write code to accomplish it. One way is to have the robot angle its side range sensor a little more forward. We want it still looking left enough to keep a steady distance from the wall, but if the wall ahead starts to turn outward, the new angle will give the robot a slightly earlier warning of the upcoming turn. Starting the turn early should help the robot handle problems like the one above.

If you use an angle of -65° for **rRange()** and go back to a distance of 50, you will get the results shown in Figure 9.9. If you compare Figure 9.8 to Figure 9.9 you can see the new algorithm is trying to work. The robot is starting to turn, but just not fast enough.

Figure 9.9: If the robot looks ahead slightly it seems to work better.

We can solve the problem shown in Figure 9.9 by telling the robot to make faster turns. The question is, will the robot still perform properly on other areas of the wall. If we change the **rTurn** statements to 2 and -2 instead of 1 and -1, you get the result shown in Figure 9.10. This time, the robot almost makes it. Note: This is like changing the **TurnStyle** on the S3. Using turns of 2 and -2 would cause the real robot to have a jerky movement.

There are several things we can try. We might make the robot turn faster or we could change the angle of the **rRange** statement, or we could increase the distance the robot stays from the wall. You might want to experiment with these options before reading further.

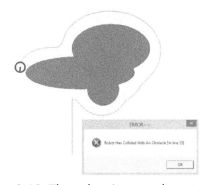

Figure 9.10: The robot is now almost perfect.

A Solution is Found

After experimenting with the parameters mentioned, I found turning ±2 with an angle of -75⁰ and a distance of 60 units seem to work well. Figure 9.11 shows the final output. Experiment on your own and see if you can improve on the robot's wall-following behavior.

Figure 9.11: The simulated robot seems to handle all situations.

Using the Real Robot

Now that we have the simulation working and have a better understanding of what a robot needs to do to follow a wall, let's port all that knowledge to the S3. Remember, since the S3 uses an ultrasonic ranger, is not exactly like the simulation. This means we may have to fine-tune some of the parameters that influence the robot's wall-following behavior, but at least we now know what things are important.

Our first order of business is to use the sub-routine **UltraSonicRange()** developed in Chapter 8 in or to better find parameters that will work with the S3. With a few tries, it was determined that the scans needed to go at least 70⁰ to the left. The beam on a Ping sensor is easily 40⁰ wide so I used **UltraSonicRange(-70,-30,R)** which puts the measured distance in the variable **R** as needed. This produced the output shown in Figure 9.12.

Figure 9.12: Simulating an ultrasonic scan works well.

The parameters used (-70,-30) implies that the center of the angled beam is 50⁰ from the forward heading. If the side Pings are mounted back 45⁰, they should still work (most Ping beams are wider than 40⁰), but our simulation tells us we could be getting into a border-line case. For that reason, the side sensors on the S3 mount are actually angled at 50⁰. This helps ensure the S3 can follow walls without problems, and the sensors are still far enough forward to help prevent forward-moving collisions. With this latest information, we are ready to try the S3.

A Real Wall to Follow

It was easy to create a shape to serve as the wall for the simulation to follow. Now that we are using a real robot, we must have a real wall for it to follow. You could use a makeshift wall made from furniture, boxes, briefcases, etc. but Figure 9.13 offers a better solution. It shows the foam board sections and cut down oat boxes mentioned in Chapter 8 laid out on the floor to create a wall. If your floor is a large white board, you could even let your S3 leave a trail as it moves.

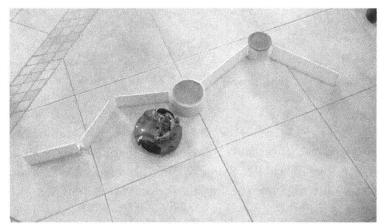

Figure 9.13: Wall modules make building real walls and obstacles easy.

Modify the programs in this chapter and verify they can make your S3 follow a real wall. Adjust pertinent parameters (*distance from wall* and *how fast the robot turns*) appropriately if the robot fails to follow the wall. Remember, the easiest way to control how fast the **S3** makes turns is with the **rCommand** that sets the *turnstyle*. Don't forget to remove the **rForward** statement as we have in similar programs from previous chapters. Using only **rTurn -1** and **+1** with an appropriate **TurnStyle** will prevent jerky movements. Try experimenting with all the options to ensure your robot can follow walls with a variety of curves.

Experiment on your own and make your S3 follow a wall. Try different parameters including distance from the wall and altering the **TurnStyle**. You might even dream up something entirely different that works too. It is very important that you try to do this on your own before looking at the solution in Figure 9.14 (which uses the default **TurnStyle** - perhaps you can do better). Remember, this is only ONE way to solve this problem. Anything that you create that works is an equally good solution.

The whole point of this exercise is to demonstrate the way you have to think and experiment in order to find appropriate ways for your robot to best use its sensors. The simulator is a huge help because it can help you understand what things are important and it can help you find parameters that have a good chance of working with the real robot. As you should expect though, additional tweaking may be required.

Note: If your S3 only has one ranging sensor, angle it to the left 50⁰ to follow the wall and use **rFeel()** with the S3's IR sensors to find the wall. Depending on the detection range of your IR sensors, you may have to have the robot move forward slightly after the robot has found the wall. Use what you have and experiment to make it work.

```
#include "InitS3.bas" // or merge it
PortNum = 5 // set to your Bluetooth Port

Main:
  gosub InitS3
  gosub FindWall
  gosub Follow
end

FindWall:
  While rRange()>10
    rForward 1
  wend
return

Follow:
  rTurn 90
  while TRUE
    if rRange(-50)>25 // any neg. # uses the left PING
      rTurn -1
    else
      rTurn 1
    endif
    //rForward 1
  wend
return
```

Figure 9.14: This is one solution for making the S3 follow a wall.

Continual Improvement

Readers that want to continue improving this algorithm might use the left Ping to follow the wall and the front Ping to watch for the need to turn right quickly. Remember, there is no right or wrong solutions. Anything is good that works.

Chapter 10
A Virtual Sensory System

Previous chapters have given you a little insight into the value ranging sensors provide for your robot. For more complex behaviors though, you typically need to obtain the distance readings from all three Pings and manipulate that information into a format better suited for your needs. The RROSS can handle this for you. The basic idea is that the ranging data from all three sensors will be used to emulate sensors your robot does not have – but sensors that the simulated robot *does have*. This will allow us to access *virtual sensors* on the S3 using the functions designed to access the simulator's sensors

Look at Figure 10.1. It represents the **rFeel()** sensors on the simulator. It is important to distinguish these *proximity* sensors from ranging sensors. The front or center sensor, for example either reports 0 (if no object is seen with a specified distance) or 4 (if something is seen within the specified distance). This information only tells us if an object is detected, not how far away it is. If you recall from Chapter 5, the S3's IR sensors are also proximity sensors. Note: You can actually purchase sensors of this type (their output is either ON or OFF depending on if an object is detected within their limited range). The detection range for proximity sensors varies based on the units you purchase. In some cases, the detection range is manually adjustable.

Figure 10.1: The simulator has five FEEL sensors.

In many cases, we don't care how far an object is from the robot. Just knowing something is in the way, within a specific range, might be all the information needed. For example, the robot might react to an object detected by sensor 2 by turning left. Of course, we could obtain the range reading from the right-side Ping and check to see if its value was less than a specified distance – but having to do that for three Pings can be cumbersome. For that reason, we will let the RROSS do that for us.

FEEL Sensors
The RROSS will obtain the three range readings and test each to see if they are less than a specified distance (more on this shortly). If the left sensor detects an object, the value of **rFeel()**

will be set to 8 and if the front sensor is triggered, **rFeel()** will be 4. If both the left and front sensors detect objects, then the sensor value will be 12 (8+4). If all three sensors detect objects, the returned value will be 14 (8+4+2). If you think about this for a moment you can see how the FEEL data can provide a lot of information in an easy-to-use format.

BUMP Sensors

The simulator also has bumper sensors that can be accessed with the **rBumper()** function. You might recall that **rBumper()** was used in Chapter 6 to access data from the **S3**'s light sensors. The simulator's bumper system is not configured exactly like the FEEL sensors, but it is close enough for our purposes.

The RROSS can provide data for **rBumper()** just like it does for **rFeel()** but it reports objects that are closer to the robot. The actual detection range will be half that of the FEEL sensors. Let's look at an example to help clarify this.

Suppose we agree on a detection range of 16cm for **rFeel()**. This means that if an object is directly in front of the robot and closer than 16cm, then **rFeel()** will return a value of 4. This will also mean that **rBumper()** will return a value of 4 if the object is closer than 8cm (16/2). This simply means you can use **rFeel()** to quickly find out if there are objects close by and **rBumper()** to see if they are really close. The numbers returned will be the same (both will report 2, for example, if an object is detected to the front-right side of the robot). The only difference is the detection distance.

A VSS

It is important to remember, that the Ping's do not actually give the **S3** real proximity sensors, but the RROSS can manipulate the range data and report it as FEEL or BUMP data. Effectively, the RROSS is creating *virtual* (a fake or fabricated concept that works like the real thing) sensors. You can still use **rRange()** when you need distance information, but the RROSS gives you far more options. Let's call this a virtual sensor system (VSS).

Turning on the VSS

As you know, **rFeel()** *normally* reports whether the **S3**'s native IR sensors detect objects and **rBumper()** is *normally* used for the light sensor data. We can use an **rCommand** to turn on the VSS and change the information provided by **rFeel()** and **rBumper()**. The actual command number to do this is 17, but you can use **SetVSSmode** if you have run the **InitS3** subroutine discussed in Chapter 8. Let's look at some examples. We can establish a FEEL distance of 16cm with this command (note: you can set any distance up to 63cm):

```
rCommand(SetVSSmode, 16)
```

If you also want **rBumper()** to report virtual data from the Pings (instead of light sensor information) you can use:

```
rCommand(SetVSSmode, Bumpers+16)
```

The above command still sets the FEEL distance to 16, but it now activates the bumpers too (with a detection distance of 8).

Normally the value of **rFeel()** generated by the **VSS** will only reflect the Ping readings. In some special cases, you might want the front reading to indicate an object if one is seen by *either* the front Ping or either of the **S3**'s IR sensors. This can actually make the front reading more reliable (IR has trouble seeing dark objects that don't reflect light and ultrasonic waves can be ineffective if absorbed by soft objects such as stuffed animals). The statements below show how to activate a dual mode that tells the RROSS to utilize both the IR and Ping information for the front FEEL sensor. If you use this mode, it makes sense that you set the Ping FEEL distance equal to the operating range for *your* **S3**'s IR sensors instead of the value 16 used in the examples. Just set up a test program and measure how far objects can be detected in the native IR mode. If you use **rBumper()** in this dual mode, the front reading will not be affected by the IR data.

```
rCommand(SetVSSmode, Dual+16)
rCommand(SetVssmode, Dual+Bumpers+16)
```

The point is that the **VSS** can be initialized in a variety of ways to serve your needs. In the native **S3** mode, the **rFeel()** function only reports objects directly in front of the robot because the IR beam width is so narrow. Now, the wide ultrasonic beams should see objects anywhere in the robot's path. And you can still use **rBumper()** to retrieve light information or, if you don't need the light data, you can have the **rBumper()** report when objects are half the distance detected by **rFeel()**. Couple this with the dual mode and you have many options available. Let's look at an example program to demonstrate how powerful the **VSS** can be.

Figure 10.2 shows the environment for the program. There are four obstacles to prevent the robot from getting to the goal (the green/light green circles on the left side of the screen). The goal and the robot will both be drawn at random positions. Also, the obstacle in the upper left of the screen will be also be sized and placed randomly (which will make various paths to the goal impossible, forcing the robot to work harder to find a path). Figure 10.3 shows the module that draws the environment. Study it to see how the randomness is introduced.

Figure 10.2: This environment is just random enough
to force the robot to find a pathway to the goal.

```
DrawEnvironment:
  circle 300,random(150),360+random(50),200+random(50),BLACK,BLACK
  circle 400,350,650,500,BLACK,BLACK
  circle 200,250,300,400,BLACK,BLACK
  circle 500,100,650,250,BLACK,BLACK
  LineWidth 10
  y=random(400)
  circle 100,50+y,150,100+y,LightGreen,Green
return
```
Figure 10.3: This module draws an environment similar to Figure 10.2.

Achieving the Goal

Think about this problem. If you were the robot, how would you find a path to the goal. First of all, let's set some ground rules. We will assume that the goal can be seen at all time. Perhaps it has a flag on it that sticks up above the obstacles. Now, how would you find the goal?

Probably you would first start walking toward the goal and continue to do so until some obstacle blocked your path. If you did not know how big the object was or what objects might be behind it, you would have to flip a coin to decide if you wanted to turn left or right. You might then follow along the edge of the object (a wall-following behavior) for a while.

Of course, the object you are trying to get around might be very large in the direction you chose to walk. This could happen in real life. If you were trying to get around a large object, and if you did not succeed in some reasonable amount of time, you might decide to turn around and try the other direction.

If you keep trying to get around the object (perhaps increasing the distance you will walk in either direction), eventually you will succeed and you can start walking toward the goal again. If you run into other obstacles, just repeat the actions previously discussed. Think about this algorithm. It might not be the most efficient plan, but it does sound like it should work. Figure 10.4 shows the simulated robot trying find its way to the goal using the technique above.

Figure 10.4: The algorithm seems to work.

94

In Figure 10.4 the robot starts towards the goal and gets blocked. It follows around that object going to the right for a short time and then tries to move toward the goal again. Again its movements are blocked and it follows the object's contour to the left this time. It gets blocked by other object, and tries left again. It almost gets around the obstacle, but gives up and tries going right. Again it gives up and tries left again, but this time it gets far enough around to find the goal. One of the things that makes this algorithm work is that the amount of time the robot follows a wall before it gets bored and changes directions is random.

Think about this. If everything is random, the robot might follow along awhile and then follow some more in the same direction. Or, it might change directions several times before eventually following one of the directions long enough to get around the blocking obstacle. Let's create a program that will control the simulated robot in this way.

Creating the Main Program

Figure 10.5 shows a main program that will get us started. It starts by drawing the environment as discussed earlier. After the robot is initialized, the variable **Found** is set to **FALSE** and a **while**-loop will continue looking for the goal while it has not been found. The actual movements to find the goal (discussed earlier) are all performed in the **LookForGoal** module. It is also the responsibility of the **LookForGoal** module to set the variable **Found** to **TRUE** once the goal is found. This action will terminate the **while**-loop when the goal is found.

```
main:
  gosub DrawEnvironment
  gosub InitRobot
  Found = FALSE
  while not Found
    gosub LookForGoal
  wend
  print "FOUND"
end
```

Figure 10.5: This main program shows *what* needs to be done to find the goal

LookForGoal

Now that we have a good overview of the program, we need to examine the **LookForGoal** module to find out *how* the robot actually finds the goal. Figure 10.6 shows the **LookForGoal** module. It starts with a **while**-loop that rotates the robot clockwise until it sees a beacon (more about the **rBeacon()** function shortly). For now, just accept that there is a beacon at the goal position.

The second **while**-loop moves the robot forward as long as an object is not blocking the path. The loop also uses the simulator's line sensors to determine if the robot has reached the goal (there is a colored area surrounding the goal that serves this purpose). If the goal is found, **Found** is set to **TRUE** and the **while**-loop is terminated early with a **break** statement. If the loop terminates because an object was blocking the path (**Found** will not be true), the module **FollowWall** is executed. All this continues until the goal is found (due to the loop in **main**). Notice the comments in the program tell you what each section does.

```
LookForGoal:
  // face the beacon
  while not rBeacon(GREEN)
    rTurn 1
  wend
  // move forward till blocked (by object or the goal itself)
  while not (rFeel()&14)
    rForward 1
    if rSense(LightGreen)
      Found = TRUE
      if Found then break // exits loop
    endif
  wend
  // if not at goal, then follow the wall randomly for a time
  if not Found then gosub FollowWall
return
```

Figure 10.6: This module gives an overview of how to find the goal.

FollowWall

The **FollowWall** routine is shown in Figure 10.7. An **IF**-statement uses random numbers to turn left or right about 50% of the time. Each of the *follow* sections (left and right) are basically the same algorithm, so only one will be discussed. When following right, the robot first turns to the right to align with the wall. If the front FEEL sensor is active (indicating a collision is eminent), the robot turns 90° to avoid it. (This would have been a nice addition to the wall-following behavior in Chapter 9.) A **FOR**-loop forces the robot to follow the wall for a random distance (between 100 and 400 pixels). The distance measured left of the robot is obtained and the robot turns left or right to maintain that distance from the wall. If nothing is in front of the robot, it moves forward slightly.

This algorithm makes the robot keep trying different paths until it finally reaches the goal. The robot will often appear to be stuck in a particular situation, but eventually it tries something a little different and makes its way to the goal.

Enter all these routines into RobotBASIC and add your own **InitRobot** routine to initialize the simulation. Test it to verify it works. See if you can modify the program to improve on its ability to find the goal.

```
FollowWall:
  // randomly go left or right
  if random(100)<50
    // go right
    rTurn 90
    if rFeel()&4 then rTurn 90
    for r=1 to 100+random(300)
      R=rRange(-60)
      if R >70
        rTurn -1
      else
        rTurn 1
      endif
      if not(rFeel()&14) then rForward 1
    next
  else
    // go left
    rTurn -90
    if rFeel()&4 then rturn -90
    for r=1 to 100+random(300)
      R = rRange(60)
      if R >70
        rTurn 1
      else
        rTurn -1
      endif
      if not (rFeel()&14) then rForward 1
    next
  endif
return
```

Figure 10.7: This routine will follow a wall for a random distance.

Converting the Program for the S3

Now that we have a working program that makes the simulation find a goal, it should be easy to modify it so the S3 will exhibit the same behavior. Before we continue though we need an S3 version of the simulator's beacon detector. Chapter 2 provides wiring and mounting information for the RobotBASIC beacon detector. Appendix B explains how to build the beacon itself. Beacon chips, kits, and beacon detectors are available from www.RobotBASIC.org.

Once you have a beacon system, try to convert the simulator program to work with the S3 on your own. If you have trouble, Figure 10.8 shows a complete program. It is not all that different from the simulator version. There are a few things worth mentioning. First, the VSS mode is being used, but you could use the S3's native IR sensors for the **rFeel()** statements. You do however need ranging sensors on the left and right if you want to follow walls in both directions.

Each time the program *looks for the goal*, it *rotates* the S3 to find the beacon. Notice the change in **TurnStyle** to allow this to happen. Once it is facing the beacon, it moves forward until the front **rFeel()** sensor indicates it is blocked. While it is moving forward, it also checks the line sensors with **rSense()** to see if it gets to the goal. If it gets blocked again during this process, it follows a wall, randomly left or right, for a random amount of moves.

Notice also that the **rBeacon()** function in this program uses a parameter of zero. This makes it return the number (1-8) of *any* beacon is sees (or zero otherwise). If you use a specific parameter, 2 for example, it will only return a non-zero value if it sees beacon number 2.

You should experiment with the random times for following the wall. For example, you might want to lengthen it if your objects are large, or reduce it if your objects are small. Depending on your environment, you might also want the robot to stop sooner when blocked or follow the wall closer or further from it.

The beacon should have multiple IR LED's so that it can be seen from various angles. Refer to Appendix B to learn more about beacons.

```
#include "InitS3.bas"
PortNum = 5

main:
  gosub InitS3
  rCommand(SetVSSmode,8)
  Found = FALSE
  while not Found
    gosub LookForGoal
  wend
  print "FOUND"
end

LookForGoal:
  // Face Goal (could face brightest light)
  rCommand(SetTurnStyle,100) // set rotating turns
  while not rBeacon(0)  // look for any beacon
    rTurn 1
  wend
  rCommand(SetTurnStyle,50)  // back to slow wheel turns
  // move forward until blocked
  while not (rFeel()&4)
    rForward 1
    if rSense() // check for dark area around goal while moving
      Found = TRUE
      if Found then break
    endif
  wend
  if not Found then gosub FollowWall
return
```

```
FollowWall:
  // randomly go left or right
  if random(100)<50
    // go right
    rTurn 90
    for r=1 to 20+random(50) // experiment with these values
      R=rRange(-50)
      if R >25
        rTurn -1
      else
        rTurn 1
      endif
    next
  else
    // go left
    rTurn -90
    for r=1 to 20+random(60)
      R = rRange(50)
      if R >25
        rTurn 1
      else
        rTurn -1
      endif
    next
  endif
return
```

Figure 10.8: This program makes the S3 find a beacon.

Creating an Environment for the S3

You can create an appropriate environment for the S3 using the walls and obstacles discussed in Chapter 9. The beacon needs to be high enough to be seen over obstacles, so set the beacon on one of the obstacles – they are a perfect height. The obstacle holding the beacon needs to have a dark floor surface around it, sticking out far enough it will be detected before the **rFeel()** sensors think the S3 is blocked again. This lets the S3's line sensors determine when the goal has been reached. Figure 10.9 shows a sample environment. Notice the piece of dark paper around the goal. Just place the robot somewhere away from the goal, as shown, and it should find its way around objects blocking its path to find the beacon.

Figure 10.9: This is a sample environment for beacon detection.

Beacon Substitution

If you have not modified your S3 for beacon detection, or you do not have a beacon, you can still program your S3 for a goal finding activity. Recall how **rLook()** can be used to find a bright light in Chapter 6. Instead of using a beacon to identify the goal, use a bright light (perhaps a good flashlight). Since this project only has one goal (you could have up to 8 different beacons), such a substitution should work fine. Of course, you will have to experiment with the light source to ensure it is bright enough and angled properly to be seen throughout the environment and over your obstacles.

A Real Challenge

This project should represent a real challenge for most readers. The problem of course is that I have no idea what your environment will be like and that means you may need to tweak the program of Figure 10.8 to make it work for you. Ideally you should be able to create a program that works for a wide variety of situations. Try not to be frustrated and don't expect a quick solution. Solving programming problems can be fun and exciting if you enjoy a challenge.

Chapter 11
Combining Behaviors: Avoiding Objects on a Line

As we have seen in previous projects, the real secret to programming is that small modules can be combined to build bigger ones and then the bigger ones can be combined to build even bigger ones etc. When this continues, the end result can be a huge program with massive capabilities that is composed entirely of small easy-to-understand blocks of code. The project in this chapter serves to reinforce these principles.

A Complex Task

In this chapter, we want the robot to follow a line until some obstacle blocks the robot's way. When this happens, the robot should abandon its line-following behavior and use wall-following to find its way around the obstacle. This means it should follows the contour of the object until it sees the line again, at which time it should return to the line-following behavior. Figure 11.1 shows what we want to happen.

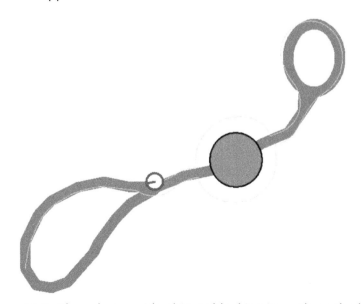

Figure 11.1: The robot avoids objects blocking its path on the line.

The robot in this example starts in the lower left hand corner and moves along the upper part of the line until it comes to the object blocking its path. Notice the robot is using the initial line-following algorithm discussed in Figure 7.3 in Chapter 7. It goes around the object and continues following the line along its right edge. Notice both ends of the line are now circular so that the robot can follow around the ends and continue following the same line back toward the obstacle.

When the robot gets back to its starting position it will take the lower path back to the obstacle and again avoid it. From then on, the robot stays on the outside of the line and switches back and forth between line-following and wall-following behaviors, as needed. A cool aspect of this program is that the robot never stops because the lines curve back on themselves. The program that produces this output (but without the line showing the robot's path) is provided in Figure 10.2.

```
Main:
  gosub DrawLine
  gosub InitRobot:
  gosub FollowLine:
end

FollowLine:
  // a modified line follow
  while TRUE
    if rRange()<10 then gosub AvoidObject
    if rSense()&1
      rTurn 1
    else
      rTurn -1
    endif
    rForward 1
  wend
return

AvoidObject:
  // basically a modified wall follow
  rTurn 90
  while not rSense(GREEN)&1
    if rRange(-75)>35
      rTurn -1
    else
      rTurn 1
    endif
    rForward 1
  wend
  rForward 20
  while not rSense(GREEN)
    rTurn 1
  wend
return
```

```
InitRobot:
  rLocate 50,500
  rSpeed 2 // slow robot down
  rInvisible GREEN
return

DrawLine:
  LineWidth 20
  SetColor GREEN
  line 50,500,50,450
  lineto 75,400
  lineto 100,375
  lineto 150,350
  lineto 200,340
  lineto 250,350
  lineto 300,350
  lineto 350,330
  lineto 400,320
  lineto 450,300
  lineto 500,270
  lineto 550,250
  lineto 600,180
  lineto 600,100
  circle 550,50,650,175
  line 580,170,578,210
  line 50,500,70,530
  lineto 100,535
  lineto 130,525
  lineto 180,470
  lineto 190,450
  lineto 220,410
  lineto 250,380
  lineto 295,355
  LineWidth 3
  circle 400,250,500,350,BLACK,RED
return
```

Figure 11.2: This program allows the simulated robot avoid objects while following a line.

The Differences

Most of the program in 11.2 is the same or very similar to what you have seen in previous chapters. Other than the **DrawLine** module, there are really only slight differences in two modules. Let's look first at the module **FollowLine**. The only change (when compared to the **FollowLine** from previous chapters) is shown in **bold** in the figure.

The new **if**-statement monitors the ranging sensor and calls **AvoidObject** when an object is detected. **AvoidObject** is basically a modified wall-follow subroutine. It has several changes when compared to the original. All three changes are in **bold** to help you locate them.

The first bold line is the **while**-statement. In the previous version, this was a never ending loop because the controlling parameter that was always **TRUE**. In this version, the loop only continues as long as the robot does not see a line. This simply means the wall-following behavior will continue until a line is found (indicating the robot has found its way around the object). When the wall-following behavior is terminated, the robot needs to align itself with the line so that the line-following behavior can resume. It does this by moving forward slightly (to get on the line) and then *rotating* to the right until the line sensors detect the line.

Alternative AvoidObject
Even if your S3 does not have wall-following capabilities, you can still work on this project by letting the robot move around the object in a circular motion without using any sensory information (except for looking for a line). Figure 11.3 shows one way of doing this. Without a range sensor to follow the contour, the arc traveled by the robot will always be the same so you have to know in advance the size of the object. Remember, when using the S3 you can alter the **TurnStyle** and easily change the arc's diameter to fit the object you use. This technique is very limited compared to following the contour (which can handle *any size object* it encounters on the line), but it is a way for non-Ping-equipped S3's to demonstrate avoiding objects while following a line.

```
AvoidObject:
  rTurn 90
  while not rSense(GREEN)
    rTurn -1   // use TurnStyle for the S3
    rForward 1 // add more forwards to make the arc bigger
  wend
return
```
Figure 11.3: This simple version of **AvoidObject** does not need a range sensor.

When using **TurnStyle** to move in an arc, you can stop the movement at any time (such as when the line is seen). The disadvantage is that you have to experiment with different **TurnStyle** values to determine exactly how big the arc is. It is also difficult to determine how far the robot will move if you are trying to make it perform an exact maneuver. The RROSS has two **rCommand**s that give you access to the S3's native capability to move in a circular manner.

Controlled Arcs with the S3
The first of these commands is **rCommand(SetHalfDriveDegrees, deg/2)**. Use a value for the variable **deg** to control how far the robot should move. If you want the robot to move in a full circle, **deg** should be 360. We have to divide the value by 2 because the maximum size of the parameters using in **rCommand**s is 255. Without the divide, you would not be able to move the

robot in a full circle. This does reduce the resolution to 2 degrees, but that is not really much of a restriction in most situations.

Once the arc length is established (it defaults to a full circle) you can use **rCommand(DriveRightCurve, radius)** or **rCommand(DriveLeftCurve,radius)** to command the S3 to start driving. The radius can be any number up to 255 and is in units of .5 inch. So, for example, the following two commands would move the robot in a counter-clockwise half circle (180⁰) with a radius of 10 inches.

```
rCommand(SetHalfDriveDegrees, 180/2)
rCommand(DriveLeftCurve, 20)
```

A Challenge
The program in Figure 11.2 is composed almost entirely of code discussed in detail in previous chapters. With the additional explanations in this chapter, you should have a good understanding of how each of the new routines work. Additionally, you now have experience converting simulator programs so that they work with a real robot.

Your challenge is to convert the program of Figure 11.2 so that it can control your S3. Study the projects in previous chapters if you have problems and experiment with various parameters to fine-tune your robot's performance so that it works to your satisfaction. Analyzing the effects of your modifications and experimenting to improve the program's performance is what programming is all about. Hopefully you will enjoy the experience. Figure 11.4 shows a reasonable environment for this challenge. Notice the object at the end of the line. You could use this second obstacle to stop the robot when it is detected or, you could have the robot turn 180⁰and follow the line in reverse.

When you are successful, turn to Chapter 12 where we will explore the topic of autonomous navigation.

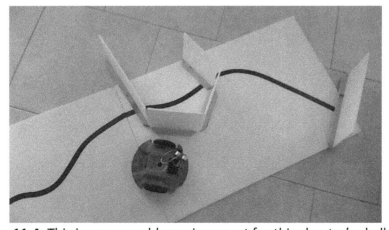

Figure 11.4: This is a reasonable environment for this chapter's challenge.

Chapter 12
Autonomous Navigation

Hopefully you have found the projects in previous chapters both interesting and challenging. This chapter is a little different though, because the topics discussed involve the real-world task of navigating through a home or other *known* environment. To be fair, it must be said that the approaches to navigation discussed in this chapter are far from state-of-the-art, but the principles examined are workable and can easily be achieved by students and hobbyists using an S3 robot.

The Goal
The goal of this chapter is to create a robot that can find its way through a home (or similar environment) without human assistance. The robot, of course, will be the S3 and that means the "home" being navigated might well be a large table or floor area with walls and obstacles made from foam board. This allows the S3 robot to validate the software we develop by demonstrating it can find its way between various positions within the specific environment.

Since this is the final chapter in this book, the finalized code will not be provided. Instead, a variety of concepts, suggestions, and examples will be examined with the expectation that the reader will apply them to their own unique project and environment.

Fixed Positions
A more ambitious project might let the robot wander freely throughout a home. Such behaviors often require an electronic compass, cameras for vision, and/or local positioning hardware and software. To make this problem manageable for the S3, we will simplify our expectations. Let's start by establishing several fixed positions in some reasonable environment and develop algorithms for moving between any of the places. While this approach might seem extremely limiting, it can serve as a very workable solution for a relatively complex problem.

A Specific Example
Look at Figure 12.1. It shows a simple floorplan that will be used in this chapter to develop navigational principles and algorithms. After you understand the concepts, you can apply them to your own environment and your S3.

An important aspect of the floor plan is the five positions depicted by numbered circles. They represent positions in the home that we might want a robot to visit. The S3 is not big enough to carry food or drinks throughout a home, but the navigational principles are the same whether you are controlling the S3 or a life-sized creation.

Figure 12.1: A realistic environment for the simulated robot.

Imagine, for example, that you are watching television and tell your robot to go to the kitchen, where someone places a sandwich and drink on a tray mounted on the robot before telling the robot to go to the living room. When it arrives, you take your food and tell the robot to retreat to the bedroom.

Consider a life-sized robot that will make its way to the front door whenever it hears the doorbell. It could greet people and invite them in if it recognizes their face. It could offer to take their coats and then move to a bedroom until summoned to bring the back.

The S3 does not have many of these capabilities, but it still makes a great tool for learning about navigation. Plus, since the S3 is controlled by a full computer (not just an imbedded micro-controller like most educational robots) adding things like voice recognition and cameras is certainly possible (see Appendix C).

Fixed Positions
As mentioned earlier, this chapter's approach to navigation is to restrict the robot's movements to specific fixed positions (labeled 1-5 in Figure 12.1). To make it easy to control the robot, we will have five buttons on the right side of the screen, as shown in Figure 12.2.

Figure 12.2: These buttons control the robot's movements.

Another way to make this program easy to write, is to assume we have subroutines that move the robot from any position to any other position. For our program, the subroutines will have the name **Move** followed by two numbers. For example, the subroutine **Move31** should move the robot from position 3 to position 1. **Move25** moves the robot from position 2 to position 5. The question now becomes, how do we know which subroutine to call?

Where We Are and Where We Are Going

We will use two variables to keep track of where the robot currently is and where we want it to go. The variable **CurPos** will hold the number indicating where the robot is. This variable will be updated every time the robot moves. For example, the last line in the module **Move23** should set **CurPos** to 3 (because that is where the robot should be when that module is finished.

The variable **Dest** will keep track of the destination position. This variable will get a new value each time a button is pressed. Let's see how we can check the buttons and get this information. The sub-routine in Figure 12.3 will wait for a button to be pressed, and then assign a value from 1 to 5 to the variable **answer** depending on which button was pressed. If we execute this routine with the command **call CheckButtons(Dest)**, then the variable **Dest** will have the value of the destination position.

Notice this module uses a new type of loop for this book (a **REPEAT-UNTIL**). This loop is similar to the **WHILE-WEND**, but it decides if the loop should quit at the END of the loop, rather than at the beginning (like the **WHILE**). This means the body of the loop will always be executed at least once. This is very important because the test to see if the loop should be exited (**LB<>" "**) would not make any sense when executing a **WHILE**, because **LB** does not have a valid value until the loop has actually executed.

```
sub CheckButtons(&answer)
  // wait for some button to be pressed
  repeat
    LB = LastButton()
  until LB<>""
  // assign a value to answer based on button
  if LB = "Bedroom 1"  then answer = 1
  if LB = "Bedroom 2"  then answer = 2
  if LB = "Kitchen"    then answer = 3
  if LB = "Living RM"  then answer = 4
  if LB = "Front Door" then answer = 5
return
```

Figure 12.3: This routine will provide the number of the
destination position based on which button is pressed.

If we assume that **CurPos** holds the value of the robot's current position, we can make a routine that can automatically call the right move routine each time a button is pressed. Such a routine is shown in Figure 12.4. All of the code is inside an endless **WHILE**-loop, so the program continually checks the buttons (by calling the routine in Figure 12.3) and executing the appropriate subroutine (by creating the **SubName** as discussed earlier). The + sign is normally used to add numbers together. When used with strings (of characters) though, it simply appends each new item to the total string. In most computer languages, you must convert numeric values to characters (which can be done in RobotBASIC) before joining them with a string. RobotBASIC is smart enough to assume that is what you are trying to do though, so it *automatically* performs all the conversion for you.

```
MoveRobot:
  while TRUE
    call CheckButtons(Dest)
    SubName = "Move"+CurPos+Dest
    gosub SubName
  wend
return
```

Figure 12.4: This routine will execute the proper routine as directed by the buttons.

This means we can created a **main** program that navigates the floorplan in Figure 12.1 as shown in Figure 12.5.

```
main:
  gosub DrawHouse
  gosub DrawPositions
  gosub CreateButtons
  gosub DrawBeacon
  gosub InitRobot
  gosub MoveRobot
end
```

Figure 12.5: This is the main routine for our navigation program.

Of course, we still need twenty *Move* routines, each of which moves the robot from one of the five positions in Figure 12.1 to one of the others. Why twenty? The robot can move to four different locations from each of the five positions (4x5 = 20). While this means we have to write many routines, the advantage is that each routine is very specific in nature and thus less complicated. This also means you can write one routine at a time, so the program seems far less complicated than it will eventually be.

To keep things simple, you could disable the buttons for positions 1 and 5 (Bedroom 1 and the Front Door). This means you only need a total of six routines as shown in Figure 12.6 to move the robot between positions 2, 3, and 4. Once you understand how to write these routines, you can test your skills by creating the necessary *Move* routines.

Each of the routines in Figure 12.6 is empty except for the required last line that sets the variable **CurPos** equal to the position of the robot after the routine is complete. The actual code for each of these routines will be totally different based on the environment used, so you should expect to write custom routines for *your* S3's situations. To help you do that though, the remainder of this Chapter will discuss the problems you will have and explore a variety of solutions you can use.

```
Move23:
  CurPos = 3
return

Move24:
  CurPos = 4
return

Move32:
  CurPos = 2
return

Move34:
  CurPos = 4
return

Move42:
  CurPos = 2
return

Move43:
  CurPos = 3
return
```

Figure 12.6: It takes six routines to move between positions 2, 3, and 4.

Problems to be Solved

There are many problems to be solved, and they all center around repeatability. Assume we have two locations that we want the robot to travel between, as shown in Figure 12.7. The lower location is 200 pixels to the right and 200 pixels below the first location. The code fragment in Figure 12.8 can move the robot from the first position to the second and back again (on a different path). The robot is assumed to be initialized with it pointing to the right. The code returns the robot to the original location and its original orientation, making it ready to perform the movement again. The distance back is calculated using the Pythagorean Theorem.

Figure 12.7: Assume we want the robot to travel between these two locations.

```
rForward 200
rTurn 90
rForward 200
rTurn 135
rForward sqrt(80000)
rTurn 135
```

Figure 12.8: This fragment moves the robot from one location to the other and back again.

If the code is executed, the robot moves along the path shown in Figure 12.9. Since the simulated robot moves very accurately, it can repeat this sequence over and over, always returning to the exact same spot. Real robots however, *always* have some amount of error in their movements.

Figure 12.9: The robot is accurately moving back to its starting position.

We can introduce error into the simulated robot using the **rSlip** command (just enter it after the robot is located). Using **rSlip 3**, for example, will produce a random error up to 3% on every movement. Figure 12.10 shows the robot completing its path with 3% error. Compare the path to that of Figure 12.9.

Figure 12.10: The movements are inaccurate when error is introduced.

If we put the code in Figure 12.8 inside a loop, and repeat it three times, we can see that the accumulating error will get larger with each new attempt. This happens because the robot starts each new pass through the loop with an offset position and heading when compared to the previous starting position.

Figure 12.11 shows how this error accumulates if the robot repeats the path three times. With 3% error the accumulation is huge. Even with only 1% error, the robot is showing significant problems. When repeating movements like this, it will not take long for the robot to become totally lost within its environment.

3% error   1% error

Figure 12.11: Each new path is worse than the last.

Movements of this kind are called *open loop*, because the robot moves without getting any feedback to help it get back on track. What we need is a way for the robot to periodically get itself close to its original position, and headed in the right direction. With such a correction, even if is not perfect, the error *will not accumulate* over time as long as the robot continues to periodically correct.

Figure 12.12 shows one method for achieving this correction. A RED line has been placed on the floor. Instead of the robot moving 200 pixels (as it did in Figure 12.8) the robot now moves until it finds the line. It then centers itself on the line pointing generally down the line and starts following the line until the line ends. This line-following action ends with the robot at the end of the line facing the next position. It might be a little off, but in general, the robot will always be pretty close to the end of the line with its heading pointing pretty much toward the target.

Figure 12.12: One method for correcting errors in the robot's movements.

Notice that by aligning with the line, the robot always ends up pretty close to the center of the lower location. When it moves to the upper location, the **SLIP** error prevents the robot from being centered on the desired position with the desired heading. As you can see from the figure, the robot heads toward the line at various angles depending on the errors from the last move. Each time the line is encountered though, the robot re-aligns itself and gets back on track. As long as the error is not large enough to make the robot miss the line, the robot should constantly correct itself (a *closed-loop* movement). Even after 50 moves between the two positions at 2% error, the robot is still on track as shown in Figure 12.13.

Figure 12.13: With a closed-loop movement, the robot constantly gets back on track.

The code in Figure 12.14 demonstrates how this new movement is achieved. Now, instead of moving 200 pixels, the robot only moves 160 to get close to the line, and then uses a loop to continue moving until the line is reached. It then moves forward 28 pixels to approximately center itself with the line, and then uses another loop to turn clockwise until one of the line sensors finds the line. The routine **FollowLineTillEnd** then gets the robot aligned with the line by the time the robot reaches the end. The robot then moves forward 110 pixels because that is the amount needed to get it from the end of the line to the next location (found by experimentation).

```
for i=1 to 50
  rForward 160
  while not rSense(RED)
    rForward 1
  wend
  rForward 28
  while not rSense(RED)
    rTurn 1
  wend
  gosub FollowLineTillEnd
  rForward 110
  rTurn 135
  rForward sqrt(80000)
  rTurn 135
next
```

Figure 12.14: This code fragment produces the actions in Figure 12.12.

The real key to the code in Figure 12.14 is the routine **FollowLineTillEnd**, which constantly aligns the robot. Look at the code in Figure 12.15. If you look carefully, this routine is slightly different that line-follow routines in previous chapters. The reason is that previous routines were designed to handle curvy lines; this one is only intended to follow a straight line. This means that once the robot centers itself, it can just move forward until it veers off the line, or until the end of the line is reached. It does not have to worry about losing the line due to large curves. Notice that the simulator's line-sensor reading is masked with **&5** so that the simulator is only using two line sensors like the S3. Of course, this routine must be customized to meet the environment you are using (distances between destinations, etc.)

```
FollowLineTillEnd:
  DONE = FALSE
  repeat
    S = rSense(RED)&5
    if S = 1
      rTurn 1
      rForward 1
    elseif S = 4
      rTurn -1
      rForward 1
    elseif S = 5
      rForward 1
    elseif S=0
      DONE = TRUE
    endif
  until DONE
return
```

Figure 12.15: This code aligns the robot as it follows the line.

Sometimes, though, you might want your robot to make movements without having a line on the floor. Can you think of other ways to re-align the robot?

Correcting with a Wall

Instead of following a line, can you imagine a wall-following algorithm that might work? Figure 12.16 shows a workable situation for our previous example. When the robot leaves the upper location, it moves forward far enough to be near the wall, then follows the wall on the left at a distance of 60 units until it is 75 units from the wall in front of it. These parameters are passed to the routine that actually follows the wall.

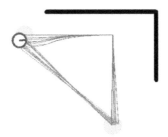

Figure 12.16: Following a wall can also re-align the robot.

In this example, the point *between* the two destinations is the most accurate. Even though the robot is never *exactly* at either of the two endpoints, it is always close, and the movement error never accumulates over time.

As discussed in previous Chapters, these routines should be modified for use with the S3. In places where the program does an **rTurn 1**, then an **rForward 1** (for example) you should eliminate the **rForward** because the S3's *turnstyle* will make it move forward as it turns. You should experiment with different *turnstyle* parameters (again, as discussed in previous chapters) to ensure the best performance from your S3. For example, when following a curvy line (and most other situations), a turnstyle of 50 is reasonable. If we are following a straight line (or straight wall) though, a higher number will make the S3 correct more slowly (and thus help ensure a better alignment).

Figure 12.17 shows a code fragment for these movements. The **FollowWallTillDone** routine performs the alignment. It allows you to specify the distance from the wall being followed as well as the distance to stop from the wall being approached.

```
for i=1 to 10
  rForward 50
  call FollowWallTillDone(60,75)
  rTurn 90
  rForward 200
  rTurn 132
  rForward sqrt(80000)
  rTurn 135
next
end

sub FollowWallTillDone(WallDist,FrontDist)
  while rRange()>FrontDist
    r = rRange(-50)
    if r<(WallDist-2)
      rTurn 1
      rForward 1
    elseif r>(WallDist+2)
      rTurn -1
      rForward 1
    else
      rForward 1
    endif
  wend
return
```

Figure 12.17: This code creates the output in Figure 12.16.

The wall-following is slightly different from previous versions because it is always following a straight wall. Previously, the robot was always turning left or right, trying to get the turn started quickly when the wall changed directions. In this code, there is a narrow margin where the robot does not try to correct. This helps ensure that the robot is parallel to the wall when it finally stops. If the robot is constantly correcting it will always be turning toward or away from the wall (thus ensuring it is not parallel with the wall).

Potential Problems

Sometimes you have a situation where the robot might get lost if is not moving as you expect. If you choose your destinations carefully, this seldom happens, but sometimes you might not have a choice. Figure 12.18 is a good example. The left-hand position (where the robot is located) is not near a wall so it has to move to a wall to obtain alignment. In this example, we want the robot to move to the upper wall and proceed as it did in the previous example. In this case though, if the robot approaches the wall a little to the left of our expectations, it could miss the corner and find itself in an unpredictable situation, as shown in Figure 12.19.

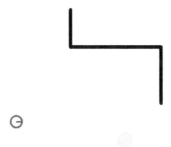

Figure 12.18: The robot can easily miss the corner without the beacon to guide it.

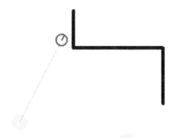

Figure 12.19: Sometimes even a small error can cause big problems.

Using a Beacon

To solve this problem, we need a way to ensure the robot stays to the right of the corner, even if its position or heading at the left-hand location is severely compromised. We can do this by placing a beacon at the corner and moving toward the beacon, staying on the right side of the beam. This allows the robot to end up in an appropriate position to move to the right and use wall following to re-align itself. Figure 12.20 shows how well this works. Notice a RED beacon

117

has been added at the corner of the wall. Refer to Chapter 10 if you need a refresher on how to use a beacon.

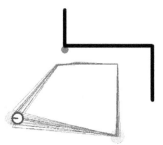

Figure 12.20: The beacon makes sure the robot arrives to the right of the corner.

Remember, the goal is to create a path that can be repeated indefinitely. In this situation, the beacon is necessary. If we used open-loop movements to get to the wall, they do work *sometimes*, but not always (depending on the robot's error, the length of the movements, etc.). Figure 12.21 shows an open-loop attempt at this pathway. The robot is successful in its first two passes, but fails on its third.

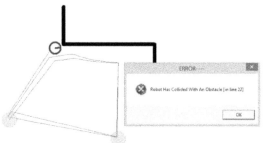

Figure 12.21: Without the beacon, the robot's error can prevent it from finding the wall.

Figure 12.22 shows a code fragment for the beacon-controlled movement. The major difference from previous examples is the module **FollowBeaconTillDone**. Notice that it allows you to pass a parameter specifying how close the robot should get to the wall before stopping.

```
for i=1 to 20
   call FollowBeaconTillDone(25)
   rTurn 45
   rForward 50
   call FollowWallTillDone(60,75)
   rTurn 90
   rForward 200
   rTurn 99
   rForward 305
next
end
```

```
sub FollowBeaconTillDone(Dist)
  while not rBeacon(RED)
    rTurn -1
  wend
  while rRange()>Dist
    if rBeacon(RED)
      rTurn 1
      rForward 1
    else
      rTurn -1
      rForward 1
    endif
  wend
return
```

Figure 12.22: This code fragment produces the movement in Figure 12.22.

As mentioned, the best solution is to choose destination positions that allow the robot to be re-aligned by following a wall or line. When this is not an option, a beacon can offer other possibilities. For hobby and educational purposes, you can probably always create a situation that does not require a beacon. Experimenting with one, however, can be both fun and enlightening.

The Program

Figure 12.24 shows all of the routines discussed in this chapter (and a few that were not discussed) assembled together to ensure clarity. As mentioned earlier, in this version, two of the buttons are disabled so that only six **Move** routines have to be written (the empty shell for each is provided).

The program even draws one beacon for you (although you might want to move it or find pathways that can periodically align the robot without using a beacon). You will also notice that the identifying numbers in the destination circles have been removed by commenting out the line that displays them. This is necessary because Windows performs font-smoothing when it displays text. What this means is that characters have extra (light-colored) pixels added around them to make curves appear smooth and round (see Figure 12.23). If look at a computer screen with a magnifying glass, you should be able to see this effect.

Figure 12.23: Extra pixels are added by windows to make characters appear smoother.

The extra pixels can make the curves seem smoother. Look at the **p**, for example, in Figure 12.23. The round corners would be very jagged if only the dark black pixels were used. The small text in the figure is the same image, only smaller. Notice how the curves appear very round and smooth.

Unfortunately these extra pixels introduce new colors to the screen – colors that are seen by the simulated robot as non-invisible obstacles. For that reason, the numbers must be removed from the destinations to allow the robot to move over them.

The program in Figure 12.24 also contains a **Coordinates** subroutine that is currently not being called from **main**. When enabled, it will not check the buttons but instead display the position of the cursor so that you can easily find positions for placing your own beacons or adding walls, etc.

```
main:
  gosub DrawHouse
  gosub DrawPositions
  gosub CreateButtons
  gosub DrawBeacon
  CurPos = 2
  //gosub Coordinates
  gosub MoveRobot
end

// you need to write these six Move routines

Move23:

  CurPos = 3
return

Move24:
  CurPos = 4
return

Move32:

  CurPos = 2
return

Move34:

  CurPos = 4
return
```

```
Move42:

  CurPos = 2
return

Move43:

  CurPos = 3
return

MoveRobot:
  while TRUE
    call CheckButtons(Dest)
    SubName = "Move"+CurPos+Dest
    gosub SubName
  wend
return

sub CheckButtons(&answer)
  // wait for some button to be pressed
  repeat
    LB = LastButton()
  until LB<>""
  // assign a value to answer based on button
  if LB = "Bedroom 1"  then answer = 1
  if LB = "Bedroom 2"  then answer = 2
  if LB = "Kitchen"    then answer = 3
  if LB = "Living RM"  then answer = 4
  if LB = "Front Door" then answer = 5
return

Coordinates:
  while 1
    ReadMouse x,y,b
    xyString 30,30,x;y;" "
  wend
return

DrawBeacon:
  LineWidth 3
  circle 255,325-11,255+22,325+11,Blue,Blue
  SetColor WHITE,BLUE
  xyString 262,325-9,"B"
  SetColor BLACK,WHITE
return
```

```
DrawPositions:
  call DrawPos(208,320,1)
  call DrawPos(208,185,2)
  call DrawPos(490,96,3)
  call DrawPos(500,325,4)
  call DrawPos(345,380,5)
return

sub DrawPos(x,y,num)
  circle x-20,y-20,x+20,y+20,LightGreen,LightGreen
  SetColor LightGreen
  xyString x-4,y-7,num
return

CreateButtons:
  SetColor Black
  xyString 722,85,"Move To"
  AddButton "Bedroom 1",715,110,80
  AddButton "Bedroom 2",715,140,80
  AddButton "Kitchen",715,170,80
  AddButton "Living RM", 715,200,80
  AddButton "Front Door",715,230,80
  // comment out these lines to use all buttons
  EnableButton "Bedroom 1", FALSE
  EnableButton "Front Door",FALSE
return

DrawHouse:
  ScrSetMetrics ,,,,0  // full screen output
  LineWidth 10
  rectangle 5,5,700,595

  xyString 60,80,"Bedroom 2"
  line 250,5,250,220
  lineto 240,220
  line 180,220,5,220
  line 245,135,195,135
  lineto 195,100
  line 195,40,195,5

  xyString 60,470,"Bedroom 1"
  line 250,595,250,290
  lineto 240,290
  line 180,290,165,290
```

```
line 245,430,195,430
lineto 195,465
line 195,555,195,595

//Bathroom
line 165,280,165,340
lineto 5,340
line 165,220,165,230
line 100,220,100,260

line 250,450,320,450
line 380,450,700,450
xyString 420,510,"Front Porch"

// doors
LineWidth 2
line 165,234,115,234
line 237,220,237,170
line 237,290,237,340
line 320,450,380,450

// counters
line 470,5,470,50
lineto 650,50
lineto 650,150
lineto 470,150
lineto 470,200
lineto 700,200

// bath fixtures
line 100,263,5,263
circle 15,228,88,259
line 5,310,90,310
lineto 90,340
circle 42,315,62,330
circle 118,298,160,317
rectangle 145,285,159,330

// furniture
LineWidth 10
line 335,62,365,62
line 335,139,365,139
LineWidth 2
circle 310,60,390,140
xyString 325,85,"Dining"
```

```
    xyString 330,103,"Table"
    rectangle 480,205,630,255
    xystring 530,225,"Sofa"
    rectangle 640,210,685,250
    rectangle 260,410,315,440
    rectangle 480,410,630,440
    LineWidth 3
    line 500,435,610,435
    xyString 544,416,"TV"
return
```

Figure 12.24: A fully-assembled version of the program discussed in the Chapter

The program in Figure 12.24 is large, so it has been included in the download for this book from www.RobotBASIC.org so that you do not have to type it in. The final assignment for this book is to create some or all of the **Move** routines so that the robot moves between locations when you press the buttons. This can be done with just the simulator, or you can create your own floorplan environment from foam board etc. so your program can control the S3.

This is certainly a difficult assignment (perhaps something suitable for a Science Fair or Computer Club Demonstration). Many readers may need to review previous chapters and modify and enhance their programs to increase their programming skills before tackling a project of this size. I wanted to include it though, to challenge more advanced readers.

Those readers with a great interest in robotics and RobotBASIC should refer to Appendix C which provides information about additional resources.

Appendix A
A RROS Overview and Advanced RROSS Options

The RROSS program is written in Parallax's BlocklyProp for the S3. Modifying this program is not a task for beginners, but advanced users can certainly alter or enhance it to meet their needs. This appendix offers a general overview of the RROSS program which should be sufficient for skilled users. This appendix is also valuable because it offers a concise summary of the RROSS's capabilities.

The RROSS

There are only a few modules in the entire RROSS program. The main program sets up communication with RobotBASIC by running the **Serin** routine as a background process (separate processor in the S3's internal *Propeller* micro-controller). **Serin** constantly watches for commands from RobotBASIC and sets the variable **OK** to **TRUE** when one has arrived. This is important, because the main program will stop the S3 motors if a new command has not been received within an appropriate period (typically 100-200 ms). This time can be altered by the user with an **rCommand**.

Commands

All commands from RobotBASIC are composed of two bytes which are stored in the variables **Command** and **Param** (one byte each). The codes for the various commands will be discussed later, but let's look at one example for clarification. If **Command** equals 6, for example, RobotBASIC is requesting the robot move forward an amount specified by **Param** which can have a maximum value of 255 (for the S3). The **Initialize** module establishes values for all the legal commands.

Processing the Command

Once a command has been received, the module **ProcessCommand** is executed. It uses a series of **IF-ELSEIF** decisions to determine which command is being requested, and then carries out that task using the value of **Param** when appropriate. The code for each of these conditions is relatively small and easy to follow if you are familiar with S3 programming. For that reason, details of this code is not discussed here.

Once a command has been processed, the RROSS always returns 5 bytes to RobotBASIC. Details for these bytes in different situations as well as command codes for controlling the S3 are provided in the RobotBASIC help file (and in many RobotBASIC books). In most cases, the data returned will be the line sensor data (**rSense**) and the **rFeel** and **rBumper** data. These items are generally very time sensitive, so the communication protocol requires that they be returned to RobotBASIC whenever an **rForward** or **rTurn** command is executed. This means this information is available *without* a formal request. Range data, in contrast, is only updated in RobotBASIC when a **rRange()** is executed, causing a formal request to be sent to the S3. This all sounds complicated, but all requests and processing of this data is handled internally and automatically by RobotBASIC. The RROSS running on the S3 simply has to process commands and return the data in the proper formats (as described in the HELP file).

Returning the Data

Once the command is processed, the main program in the RROSS has to obtain and format the appropriate information and send it back to RobotBASIC. The code for this is more complicated than you might imagine because the data sent is based on the mode. In the native mode, for example the **rFeel** data is simply the S3's IR readings (formatted appropriately). If the VSS has been initiated, the **rFeel** and sometimes the **rBumper** data are calculated from the readings from 3 Ping sensors (and the S3's light sensors in some modes). If you study the rest of this appendix (which summarizes the various modes etc.), the RROSS code for these processes should be easy to follow.

At this point the 5 bytes are returned to RobotBASIC. In some cases, the S3's motors are still running and will continue to do so unless no command is received within the timeout period (normally 100 ms). This helps ensure that the S3 moves smoothly. Motor movements are further enhanced with *turnstyle* options (discussed throughout this book) and by ramping up and down the motor speeds when such actions are helpful without compromising the accuracy of the S3's movements.

Main RROSS Commands

The primary commands (and their command codes) issued by RobotBASIC are listed in Figure A.1. The use of each of these commands is discussed throughout this text.

Command	Code
Locate	3
Forward	6
Backward	7
Turn Right	12
Turn Left	13
Range Right	192
Range Left	193
Beacon	96
Look Right	49
Look Left	48

Figure A.1: These are the primary command codes for the S3.

126

rCommands

There are many **rCommands**, many of which were discussed throughout this text. The ones that were not discussed are considered more suitable for advanced users and thus were not explored. The purpose of **rCommands** is to set up modes or to initiate actions or request data that is not otherwise available. The file InitS3 (discussed in the text) establishes the values for each of these commands and constants as shown in Figure A.2.

Command	Value	Default
SetTurnStyle	1	50
SetSpeed	2	50
DriveRightCurve	5	provide .5 inch radius
SetHalfDriveDegrees	8	360 (how far to drive)
PixelMultiplier	9	1 (2 doubles range data)
DriveLeftCurve	10	provide .5 inch radius
PlaySound	11	provide freq (/ by multiplier)
CalibLineSensors	14	rotates robot (over line)
SetFreqMult	15	10
SetDur	16	50 (500 ms, units of 10ms)
SetVSSmode	17	cm units for Feel sensors
SetTMout	18	20 (units of 10ms gives 200ms)
ReadPings	19	1st 3 bytes, in cm units
ReadAnalog	20	2 readings, two bytes each, MSB first
ReadLight	21	1st 4 bytes contain light data
ExpandFeel	22	0, set to 1 to expand Feel with digital sensors
SetBumpDist	23	normally half of Feel Distance
Bumpers	128	parameter for VSS
Dual	64	parameter for VSS

Figure A.2: These commands and constants make using **rCommands** easy.

Let's look at each of these items individually to see how and why they are used.

SetTurnStyle

For example, **rCommand(SetTurnStyle, 70)** will make the slow wheel (when executing an **rTurn 1** or **rTurn -1**) travel at 70% of the fast wheel. Using this (as described in the text) produces a much less jerky motion when moving the S3 in a circular manner. Using a parameter of 0 will cause the slow wheel to stop, and a parameter of 100 will make the robot perform normal rotational turns. For turns other that 1 and -1, the robot will always use rotational turns.

SetSpeed

The **rSpeed** command used for the simulator does not affect the S3. Use **rCommand(SetSpeed, param)** to set the S3's speed where **param** can be anything from 0 to 100 and indicates a percentage of the maximum speed.

DriveRightCurve
DriveLeftCurve
SetHalfDriveDegrees

You should first set the degrees to travel unless the default value of 360 is wanted. The number of degrees should be divided by 2, because of the limit of 255 (**param** is a byte). You can then drive either clock-wise or counter-clock-wise using the other commands (**param** controls the radius with units of .1 inch). The following lines will make the robot drive in an S shape with a radius of 5 inches for each curve.

```
rCommand(SetHalfDriveDegrees, 180/2)
rCommand(DriveLeftCurve, 50)
rCommand(DriveRightCurve,50)
```

PixelMultiplier

Normally **rRange()** returns the distance measured in centimeters. This is what most people want, but if you are trying to make a program on the simulator work with minimal modifications, it can be valuable to have the units used by the S3 try to approximate that of the simulator. For example, if the simulator measured a distance of 40 the cm distance would be approximately the diameter of the simulated robot by multiplying it by 2. Issuing the command **rCommand(PixelMultiplier, 2)** will make the S3 return a reading more like that of the simulator (doubles the number of centimeters read).

SetDur
SetFreqMult
PlaySound

The S3 can play tones. You can set the duration (units of 10ms with 500ms being the default). Play the actual tone with **rCommand(PlaySound, param/10)** where **param** is the desired frequency. This division is necessary due to the byte size in order to get reasonable frequencies. If you would rather use a different divisor for the frequency, you can use **rCommand(SetFreqMult, 10)** but substitute your preference for the default value of 10).

SetTMout

Normally RobotBASIC should communicate with the S3 in well under 200ms. If a program terminates with an error, communication ceases, and the S3 will automatically stop all motors after the timeout period. If this did not happen, errors could leave the S3 running wild. If your program is doing a lot of time-consuming things, you can set a new timeout period with

rCommand(SetTMout, 20). Since the units for this command are 10ms, this will set the default of 200ms. Substitute your preference for 10. Doing this can ensure that motors left running will continue until the next communication is received if your program is perform lengthy calculations. Do not confuse this command with the RobotBASIC command **SetTimeOut** which controls the timeout period for RobotBASIC, not for the RROSS.

SetVSSmode
SetBumpDist
Bumpers
Dual

The S3 normally uses its native IR data for the **rFeel()** function and the light sensor data for **rBumper()**. You can request **rFeel()** to return perimeter sensor information based on three Ping sensors using the limit specified in the command (maximum of 63cm). For example, **rCommand(SetVSSmode,10)** will set the proper bit in the returned data if a Ping detects something within 10 cm. If the **param** is **10+Bumpers**, then bits in the **rBumper()** data if the Pings detect something at half the distance of the *feel* parameter (5 in this example). If the **param** is **10+Dual**, the forward-facing Ping sensor will set its bit if either it or the native IR sensors detect an object. To be affective, you should use a distance approximately equal to the detection distance of your S3's IR sensors in the current environment. You can perform both of these actions with a **param** of **10+Dual+Bumpers**. In all of these examples, you can, of course, specify any distance *less than* 64. If you would prefer more control over the bump distance (rather than using half of the feel distance), you can set it with **rCommand(SetBumpDist,5)**, for example. Note: This command must be issued *after* the **SetVSSmode**. Range for the bump distance is anything from 0 to 255.

CalibLineSensors

Issuing an **rCommand(CalibLineSensors, 0)** will make the S3 rotate 360° and take numerous reading from the line sensors. If a line is detected during this motion, the S3 will use the readings take to improve on the accuracy of detecting the line used. The performance of this command is determined by internal programming on the S3 and at the time of this writing, it is not as valuable as you might expect. Hopefully, Parallax will improve on this in the future. In the meantime, try to have flat black lines with the most contrast as possible with a white surface.

ReadPings

If you need to read all three Pings, you could use three **rRange()** statements, but that can take three communication periods with the S3. Issuing an **rCommand(ReadPings, 0)** will make the S3 read all three and return them in the first 3 bytes of the 5 bytes of returned data. Since bytes are used, the data for each Ping will be maximized at 255cm. You can extract these 3 pieces of information into an array using the following code fragment.

```
Dim Pings[3]
d = rCommand(ReadPings,0)
for p = 0 to 2
    Pings[p] = ascii(SubString(d,p+1,1))
next
```

ReadLight

This is similar to **ReadPings** except that it returns information from the S3's native light sensors. The first three bytes will be the data from each of the 3 light sensors. The fourth byte will be be 4, 2, or 1 indicating which of the three sensors is seeing the brightest light. This information can be extracted in a manner similar to that described for **ReadPings**.

ReadAnalog

This is also similar to ReadPings except that it returns the data from the S3's analog pins on the hacker port. The first two bytes will be the data for Analog Port, A1 (MSB first). The next two bytes hold the data for A2. The code fragment below shows how to extract this information.

```
Dim AnalogData[2]
d = rCommand(ReadAnalog,0)
for p = 0 to 1
    HighByte = ascii(SubString(d,(p*2)+1,1))
    LowByte  = ascii(SubString(d,(p*2)+2,1))
    AnalogData[p] = HighByte*256+LowByte
next
```

RROSS Customization

It is expected that advanced users might want to customize the RROSS to meet special needs. To help you get started, two examples of improvements are described below.

ExpandFeel

The simulated robot has 5 FEEL sensors and the S3, even with VSS, only has 3. In some situations, navigating a maze, for example, you might want to have the side FEEL sensors (values 1 and 16). It is easy to add two digital sensors for this purpose as shown in Figure A.3. These sensors have some minimal adjustability as to their detection distance and are available from RobotBASIC. Connect the outputs from these sensors to the analog inputs on the S3 (right side to A0). When the analog reading is below 100, the sensor is on.

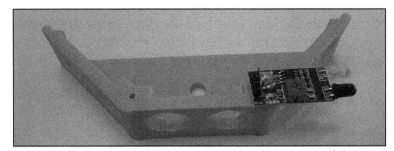

Figure A:3: Digital side sensors can be mounted on the corners of the Ping mount.

rCompass

This customization requires adding an external processor but giving the S3 a compass might make it worth the effort. The idea is simple, program the external processor to read the data from an electronic compass such as the HMC5883 and generate an analog voltage to the S3 using a D/A converter. This output voltage should be approximately 0-3.59 volts representing 0-359 degrees (i.e. a compass reading of 180° should generate a voltage of 1.8 volts. Some calibration of the output voltage is to be expected. For example, program the external processor to generate 1.8 volts and see what the S3 is returning for the **rCompass()** reading. If the reading is 175, for example, (not 180 as it should be) then increase (or decrease if the number is too high) the voltage generated. Not for beginners, but certainly an interesting project.

Implementation

In both of the above situations (**ExpandFeel** and **rCompass**), you could use these sensors by just reading the analog ports using the **rCommand, ReadAnalog**, discussed earlier. The RROSS source code, however, has them implemented into RobotBASIC for you. Study the code if you are interested in how these commands work, or to see how you might implement your own RROSS extensions utilizing the S3's A/D pins.

You can have the digital side sensor values automatically added to either the IR or Ping sensor readings returned by **rFeel()** by executing the following statement: **rCommand(ExpandFeel, TRUE)**. You can obtain a compass heading (assuming you have implemented an external processor and compass as described above) with commands like **heading = rCompass()**.

It is important to remember that these commands are not needed for the projects in this book nor for most users of the S3 robot. They are provided for advanced users and to demonstrate how new commands can be added to the RROSS.

Appendix B
RobotBASIC Beacons

A beacon detector can be an extremely useful navigation tool. Our book *Robot Programmer's Bonanza,* for example, describes in detail how to navigate through a home or office environment using strategically placed beacons. *Robots in the Classroom* shows how a robot with a compass can triangulate on two beacons to find its position in a room, thus creating a Local Positioning System (LPS). Many interesting projects can be considered if you have one or more beacons. Refer to Chapter 10 for information on how to detect beacons with the S3.

What is a Beacon

In general, a beacon can be anything a robot can locate and face. The RobotBASIC simulated robot uses colors to represent its beacons. Such an idea may sound strange, but robots with a camera can actually use disks of unusual colors for it beacons. The S3's RROSS, however, interfaces with a special sensor capable of detecting infrared light pulsing at 56kh, which means all our beacons must be oscillating at that frequency. In order to create 8 different beacons, we will have each beacon periodically turn off its signal for a short time as shown in Figure B.1.

Each beacon will generate a 56kh infrared signal for a repeating period of approximately 15ms. This time is indicated in the Figure as the ON TIME. This time period is not critical, but something close to 15ms is needed.

Each beacon will have an OFF TIME composed of a fixed initial offset plus a unique time associated with each Beacon. The RROSS assumes the unique time for Beacon #1 is 500 microseconds, Beacon #2's is 1000 microseconds, Beacon #3's is 1500, etc.

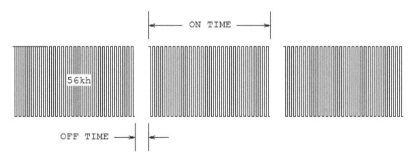

Figure B.1: Each beacon generates this waveform.

Beacons can be built in many ways, the easiest of which involves programming a small micro controller to generate the frequency patterns shown in Figure B.1. The timing for beacons is

VERY sensitive so RobotBASIC offers a preprogrammed Beacon IC that handles all the timing issues, making it easy to build your own beacons (See Figure B.2). More on this later.

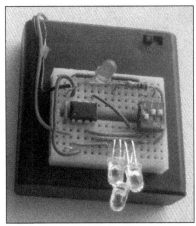

Figure B.2: Our preprogrammed chip makes it easy to create your own beacons.

Each beacon will drive one or more IR diodes depending on your application. Multiple diodes may be required to ensure visibility from a variety of angles. You might want a beacon to be visible from nearly 360º, for example, if you hang it in a doorway between two room, and want the robot to see it from any position in either room. Now that we know what a beacon is, we need a way to detect it.

The RROSS Beacon Detector

The RROSS assumes you are using the Vishay TSOP341 (Pololu #837) as the beacon detector, as shown in Figure B.3 and discussed in more detail in Chapter 2.

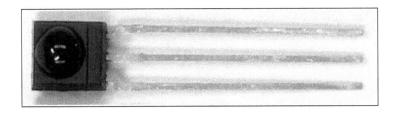

Figure B.3: This small device serves as a beacon detector.

Making Your Own Beacons

Figure B.4 shows the basic pin out for the beacon chip. You may use it to drive one or many IR LEDs. When driving only one or a few LEDs for experimental purposes, you can connect directly to the chip itself and obtain a distance of about 5 feet. If you need more LEDs and/or more distance you can use a transistor and drive multiple groups of LEDs as shown. The lower the current rating of your LEDs, the more you have to place in series to prevent burn-out, but the chip has been designed to work as shown with almost any IR LEDs. The use of transistors and higher current LEDs obviously will provide the greatest distances (typical maximums of 8-10 feet). If longer distances are required, you may need a lens of some sort to focus and direct the beam.

Figure B.4 also shows an optional standard visible LED to serve as an ON/OFF indicator – very handy especially if you tend to forget to turn your beacon off while experimenting. The figure also shows +V for all the power connections. While you can use a 5V supply, the chip allows you to power it with either 3 standard 1.5V batteries in series, or 4 rechargeable cells. Using batteries often makes sense if you are going to be moving the beacons around.

The number of LEDs you need will depend on your use of the beacon. If your robot will always be starting from approximately the same position then you might get by with a single LED. If you want your robot to see the beacon from anywhere in a room, then you need to create a light source composed of multiple LEDs mounted at different angles to produce a wide beam. Also, the height of the beacon should be similar to the height of the beacon detector. As mentioned earlier, the beacon chip can drive a few LED's directly. If you need many though, a transistor buffer should be used (see Figure B.4)

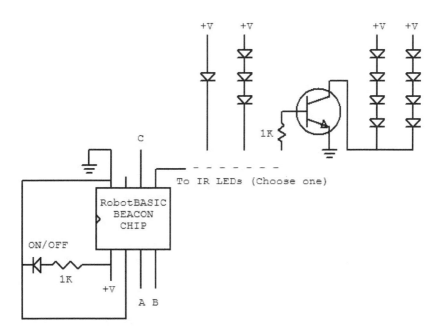

Figure B.4: The RobotBASIC Beacon Chip makes it easy to build your own beacons.

Beacon Numbers
The pins labeled A, B and C in Figure B.5 can be used to set a binary number indicating which beacon to create. Just ground a pin to make it 0 and leave it unconnected to make it a 1. These pins are constantly monitored by the internal firmware and when changed, a new beacon number is implemented immediately.

The table in Figure B.5 shows what beacon number will be created when pins ABC are connected as indicated. Most hobby and educational projects will probably use only one or two beacons so the limit of 8 different numbers should not be a problem.

A B C	Beacon #
0 0 0	8
0 0 1	1
0 1 0	2
0 1 1	3
1 0 0	4
1 0 1	5
1 1 0	6
1 1 1	7

Figure B.5: RobotBASIC beacon chips allow you to create 8 unique beacons for the S3.

Constructing Beacons

Our beacon chips make it easy to construct your own beacons as the examples in Figure B.6 shows. The beacon on the right uses a solderless breadboard. The one on the left uses a solder-based prototyping board.

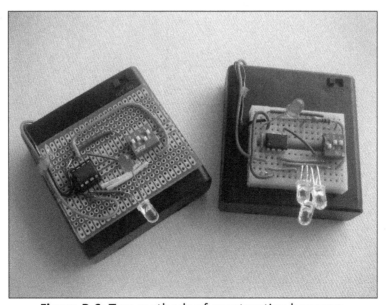

Figure B.6: Two methods of constructing beacons.

The circuits for both beacons are mounted (using hot glue or double-sided tape) on battery boxes that hold 4 AA cells. The boxes have integrated switches for turning them on and off.

The 4-gang boxes makes it easy to use 4 rechargeable cells. If you wish to use standard AA batteries (of which you should only use 3 to get an acceptable voltage) just tightly wrap an appropriately sized wooden dowel (including the ends) with tinfoil and insert it as the 4th battery. It can also be helpful to wrap tape around the battery leaving only the ends exposed.

In most cases you never need to change the beacon number of the beacons you use (just tell the RROSS what beacons you are using), so when you make a beacon you can just select its number by wiring the appropriate pins to ground. If you are always experimenting with different beacon numbers (why?), a small DIP switch can make it easy to change the beacon number. Just connect each switch between a control pin and ground. When the switch is open the pin will act as a 1 and when the switch is closed (ON) the pin will be a 0. Most users will be happy *without* a switch.

Visit the RobotBASIC webpage to purchase beacon detectors and beacon chips. Depending on demand, complete beacon kits may be available.

Appendix C
Resources

Free and almost Free

One easy and totally free option for continuing your studies is to read the RobotBASIC HELP file. It provides hundreds of pages describing the commands and functions available in RobotBASIC. You will quickly find that the material in this book barely scratches the surface of what RobotBASIC can do. On your first read through the file, don't try to understand every detail. Instead, try to discover the big picture by learning the types things RobotBASIC is capable of. Later when you are writing your own programs, you only need to remember that there was a command or function that can help you accomplish your goal. At that point you can look up the details and write some test programs to verify your understanding of the specifics before actually trying to use something new in a big program.

Another great way to study coding is to read through some of the many example programs provided in the free download of RobotBASIC. Note, the example programs are in the large main download, not the smaller download that is specific for the S3. You might also want to watch some of the many YouTube videos that provide information on RobotBASIC's capabilities (search YouTube for RobotBASIC).

If you are really interested in Robotics, consider subscribing to *Servo Magazine*. It is the premier publication for hobby robotics. I personally have published dozens of articles in Servo demonstrating various aspects of RobotBASIC and subscribers have instant access to historical issues so you will be able to read them all.

If you want to build your own robot, RobotBASIC offers a special chip with and expanded version of the S3's RROSS called the RROS (**R**obotBASIC **R**obot **O**perating **S**ystem). The RROS system can support more sensors and capabilities that were covered in this text. Robots built with RROS chips can use a wide variety of motors and sensors and are easily customized to meet your needs. The least expensive way to learn about RROS-based robots is to download a free PDF of the *RROS User's Guide* from the RROS tab at www.RobotBASIC.org.

Books on RobotBASIC

Hopefully you are able to find everything you need or want to know from the abundance of free resources for RobotBASIC. If you want to delve even deeper into some particular subject there are an abundance of books available to provide the information. If you can achieve your goals with our free materials, that's great. If you decide to buy some of our books to help support our efforts to provide support for RobotBASIC, then we thank you.   Below are general descriptions of some of the books available on Amazon.com. Most are available in print and as low-cost ebooks. Schools can contact me directly through www.RobotBASIC.org for quantity discounts.

If you look up any of these books on Amazon, you can view a detailed description of their content, access reviews from RobotBASIC users, and read sample text to help you decide if the book might be what you want or need.

These are only some of our publications and the list is constantly growing. Search Amazon.com to see everything that is currently available.

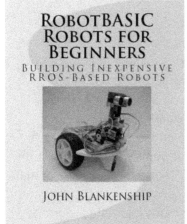 If you want to build your own robot (something similar to the S3 but far less expensive) this is what you need. It provides step-by-step details on both construction and programming.

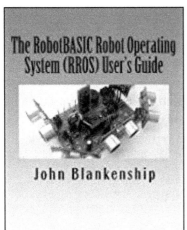 The RROS Manual is free for download on the RROS tab at www.RobotBASIC.org, but a printed version is preferred by many readers. It provides details of everything the RROS can do as well as many example programs. It is not written for beginners, but supplies a massive amount of information about building RobotBASIC robots using the RROS.

 RobotBASIC's help file is integrated into the language, but a printed version is available to those wanted the convenience to read it anywhere at any time. You could print out the help file, but it will need a lot of reformatting and probably use an entire ink cartridge.

 If you want to learn more about hardware and how sensors and motors can be controlled from RobotBASIC programs, then this is a good place to start. You will also be introduced to vision, speech, voice recognition and interfacing with microprocessors.

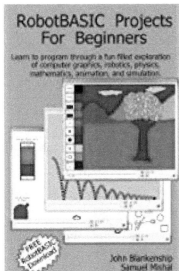 This book will teach you about programming by writing simple animations, simulations, video games, and other graphical applications. If you are a beginner and want to learn about programming, this book is our number one recommendation. The projects will make you love programming.

 This book teaches you about programming like the above book, but all of the example programs are robotic related.

This book provides more details about developing algorithms for robotic behaviors than any RobotBASIC publication. Nearly everything is done with the simulator so learning how to program a robot will never be easier or less expensive.

This is one of our most advanced books and definitely not for beginners, but if you really want to learn how to build a real robot, this is for you. Arlo is a mobile robot with two arms, vision, speech, voice recognition, an animated face, and much, much more. It is built on the RROS system so S3 users should find it an easy transition to a much more complex robot. Many of the principles discussed for Arlo will apply to the S3.

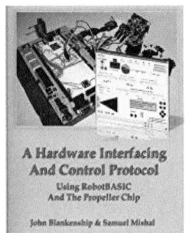

This is another of our advanced books. It provides programs that interface with a variety of sensors and the Parallax's Propeller processor (used internally for the S3). If you are a Propeller fan, you need this book.

Hopefully these resources will help you expand your skills and knowledge of robotics. Learning to program can be fun and exciting but it also develops critical thinking and problem solving skills that can carry over into many aspects of your life and help prepare you for careers in programming, engineering, and mathematics. If you love science and technology, you should learn to program.